Fly High!

by

Maria Rivera

D1707418

The Flying Cows Series:

Daring You to Soar Free

THE FLYING COWS

To my son and daughter,
because you inspire me every day

Fly High™

Author photo: Harrison Hurwitz
Editor: Laura Didyk
Book Cover Design: LSDdesign

Visit the author website: theflyingcows.com

ISBN: 978-1-7325522-0-3 (Paperback)
ISBN: 978-1-7325522-1-0 (Kindle)
ISBN: 978-1-7325522-2-7 (ePub)
ISBN: 978-1-7325522-3-4 (Audio)

Version: 2018.09.9

Published by The Flying Cows

THANK YOU …

… to the people who heard my story and asked me to write a book. Although I tried desperately to ignore your requests, I eventually realized that there was a bigger ask from me. So, thank you.

… to all the people who read and reread my writing and were willing to test the practices I outlined to ensure they worked for others. Your patience and willingness have been invaluable.

… to Winslow Eliot, my writing coach, with whose help I was able to overcome my mental blocks and all the "could not's" in my head. If not for her, this book would not exist.

… to my "amigos," my true friends, you are not only my constant cheerleaders, you are my soul family. If not for you, I would not have the courage to openly share in this book so much of my life. Your encouragement gave me the strength to be vulnerable, own my story, and stand tall.

… to my parents because they are role models of hard work and perseverance. To my late grandmother, because every time I struggled with my writing and wanted to quit, I could hear her words in the back of my head telling me that "when you are in the middle of the dance floor, you have to dance, even if your feet hurt."

Contents

Fly High!

1

I Dared to Herd Cows as a Child. Then, They Dared ME—To Fly!

When I was four years old, my parents trusted me with our most prized possessions: our cows. My daily job was to guide our seven cows to the pastures with the freshest grass. Sometimes these fields were two or three miles away from home.

I was a skinny little thing, with legs that looked like twigs. Yet with only the assistance of a big stick, I herded the cows to their destination without any problem. Somehow, I managed to keep them together when we crossed paths with other animals. Somehow, I made sure they didn't eat the neighbor's fresh corn or take a bite from a neighbor's vegetable garden. And, somehow, I got them back home before dark—all on my own.

We lived in a tiny farming town in northern Spain and we were very poor. My parents worked the fields from sunrise to sundown. All we had were a couple of pigs, some chickens, and our cows. We lived in an old stone house that had been built by my great-grandfather, and we worked fields owned by distant family members who had moved to other countries, fleeing a life of poverty and social unrest under Franco's dictatorship.

In those days, all we owned were the animals, and our lives revolved around them. They were such an important part of the household that we shared our home with them. The animals lived on the ground floor and we lived right above them. The only thing that separated us was a floor of wooden planks.

While the animals played a key role in our daily lives, the cows were at the center of everything we did. We depended on them for help in working the fields, carrying the harvest home, and as a source of money from the sale of their milk and occasionally one of their calves. The cows were our partners and our providers. Because of them, we never went to bed hungry—there was always a cup of creamy fresh milk to fill our bellies.

But my relationship with the cows went much deeper. I had no siblings and no toys, and I was the only child in the town. The family cows became my playmates and, at times, my confidants. When we were out in the fields, I would invent games for us; I would sing to them; I would pet and scratch their heads where they liked it most—right between the horns. I would engage in long conversations with them about what I was thinking, including all the things I wanted to do when I grew up. My cows were great listeners, and by looking into their eyes I understood what they were saying to me. I felt supported and nurtured by them.

Our connection was so deep that I always knew when they were happy, hungry, sick, tired, or heartbroken when a baby had been taken away. They were much more than farm animals. My cows were my best friends.

It Was an Idyllic Childhood—for a While

Many people might classify that chapter in my life as one of scarcity, limitation, and loneliness. But I never wished for anything different. I never laid awake, obsessing about what the next day was going to bring. I never hid under the covers, biting my nails in fear of the dark. I would fall asleep hearing the peaceful breathing of the cows just below my bedroom floor. It was a beautiful feeling to know that my best friends were so nearby. I would doze off with a smiling heart—at peace and filled with joy.

And every single night, I would dream my favorite dream: that my cows could fly!

In my dreams, my cows weren't cow angels with wings or cartoonish versions of cow airplanes. My cows were just themselves in their natural form, without any alteration, each a different color, size, age, and personality, jumping from cloud to cloud, and mooing with delight.

In my dreams, they would run freely through the sky, frolicking with each other, kicking their heels up to the heavens. They would play and bump into each other as if they were bumper cars up in the clouds. My cows were silly and playful, without any inhibitions, and without a care in the world.

My cows were so happy.

This beautiful dream stayed with me until the age of eight. Then one day everything changed abruptly—and my flying cows went away.

My parents had the opportunity to move to the United States. They had almost no schooling, and they didn't speak any English, but their desire for a better life pushed them to risk everything and leave their home. I found out later that they sold my cows to pay for their plane tickets.

For a long time, I didn't understand what had happened. All I knew was my cows were gone. Then, one day, my father dropped me off at a grim, dark building that looked like a prison. He handed me over to a harsh, unsmiling nun and turned around and walked away with tears in his eyes and without saying goodbye or even giving me a hug.

I felt overwhelmed with questions, but was given no answers.

What had I done so wrong to be sent away to live with these women in dark gray habits who never smiled? Why was I locked up behind dull cinder block walls, where I couldn't run free across the green meadows? Why did I have to wear this blue-and-white striped uniform, with the number four embroidered right by my heart? Was this some sort of branding, which I had seen on some cows before? Who were all these other girls, without any sparkle in their eyes? Were they being punished, too?

Who was taking care of my cows now?

The experience of sudden, heartbreaking loss—loss of everything I'd known up until then—marked me in many ways. It influenced all the turns I've made for the rest of my life. It drove me to extraordinary achievements and epic failures.

On the positive side, it prepared me to overcome every roadblock I encountered, from the time at the convent to my climb up the corporate ladder, to ultimately making it to an executive-level job in a large financial services company in the United States.

Unfortunately, it also influenced what I considered important and how I defined happiness. Perfectionism was a standard I could never meet, and self-criticism was my constant companion. Relationships tended to end abruptly. Material security mattered more than joy.

In order to endure many painful episodes in my life, I sought out every type of assistance I could find: physical, mental, emotional, spiritual, metaphysical. If it exists, chances are that I've tried it. I read self-help books. I signed up for classes. I even traveled all over the world, seeking all kinds of conventional and unconventional healers and teachers. I learned a lot and tried many things. But, while I made progress and things improved, I didn't get the lasting and heartwarming results I sought.

One Night, My Childhood Dream Returned…But Why?

And then one night, several decades after my cows disappeared from my life, everything changed again. My childhood dream of the flying cows returned!

I had not been reminiscing about my childhood. I had not been in contact with cows. I had not even thought of my cows. Yet out of the blue, there they were, just the same as when I was a child, jumping from cloud to cloud in delight, frolicking with each other, kicking their heels up to the heavens.

I woke up laughing out loud about what I had just experienced.

The next morning, I told my son and daughter about it and they teased me. It was worth a few laughs, we thought.

But, the following night, the dream came back again, and every night after that. I couldn't understand what was going on. Here I was, a grown woman, dreaming about flying cows!

The dream returned and kept returning. Sometimes I'd even dream it two or three times each night. While the dream itself was wonderful, I couldn't understand why I kept having it. I wondered what was going on in my subconscious, that after so many years, a forgotten childhood dream was now part of my nightly routine. I consulted with friends and I read up on dream interpretations. I found a lot of explanations, but none that helped me, personally.

Frustrated and confused, I consulted with my therapist about my dream. I worried there was something from my childhood that I had blocked and needed to remember. But as we talked through the dream, she asked me why I thought the cows were flying but I wasn't. She asked if they were trying to teach me something.

Then I remembered words and phrases that came to me from the cows:

They began with the word *"Dare."*

Then, *"Dare to fly."*

Then, *"Dare to rise above the clouds."*

And finally, *"Dare to elevate yourself to a new way of life."*

I realized the flying cows were inviting me to soar free, to let go of all the things that kept me weighted, burdened. Happiness and joy are found in a state of lightness of being—when we are free from the matters that make our hearts heavy. The cows encouraged me to unload all the heavy stuff that kept me chained to my past, shackled to an old way of life.

There were seven of them, and each one was showing me a different practice:

F – Flip Your Focus Inward and Challenge External Models of Dos and Don'ts

L – Listen to Your Heart—It's Hungry for Attention!

Y – Yank the Plug on the Itty-Bitty-Shitty Committee

H – Honor the Light Within Yourself

I – Inspire Your Inner Child to Come Out and Play

G – Grow High-Caliber Relationships—They Matter!

H – Help Others Soar Higher

These practices changed my life. Before I knew it, I was feeling, thinking, and behaving differently. Within a year, I sold my house on the East Coast and moved across the country. I left behind people who dimmed my light.

I left my high-paying job of twenty years to pursue my passion: to make this world a better place by helping others reach their highest potential, and to fly high!

FLY HIGH became the method that changed my life and can also change yours.

The seven practices presented in this book have helped many people create better circumstances for themselves. By making the seven practices part of their daily lives, they have found the internal fortitude and empowerment to rise above their personal challenges to achievements they never thought possible.

Here are some examples of how the Fly-High Method has helped people:

- One *Fly-Higher* earned her law degree despite her dyslexia.

- Another forgave his parents for the mistreatment he received as a child and the related damage that resulted in his relationships that came after.

- A friend of the FLY-HIGH Method finally left a toxic relationship in which she was physically and emotionally abused, and now feels confident about creating her own future.

- One middle-aged businesswoman was able to overcome the internal battles triggered by an unwanted divorce that left here feeling, according to her, "broke and broken."

- A young man found peace after a debilitating medical diagnosis and now dares to live life to the fullest.

- After many failed attempts, another Fly-Higher broke free from the golden handcuffs of a job that had him stressed, anxious, angry, and living in constant fear.

- And still another expressed gratitude for how the Fly-High practices helped her find joy again—and "heal from the inside out" after her daughter died. She has also found ways to channel her loss to help others with theirs.

Like these courageous and determined Fly-Highers, you can create an amazing personal and professional transformation for yourself.

2

How the Fly-High Method Can Help You

Have you been trying to break free from a toxic relationship, a dead-end job, unhealthy habits, patterns from your past that cause unhappiness, or people who suck the life out of you? And no matter what you try, nothing works?

I know what that feels like. I have been there many times.

But not anymore.

Thanks to the guidance of my seven cows, I went from being stuck in a constant state of fear, shame, and guilt to finding inner peace and joy; from feeling paralyzed by back-to-back failures to finally winning at the game of life; from feeling trapped in constant soap-opera-like drama, surrounded by people who were bent on hurting me and even destroying me, to only having people in my life who love me and want the best for me; from feeling powerless, hopeless, and purposeless to feeling strong, empowered, and fulfilled.

The guidance of the seven cows changed my life for the better, and it can do the same for you.

I have organized the same guidance that had such a profound impact on my life in a way that can be easily learned and used to help improve your life. I refer to it as the Fly-High Method. This method is the antidote to "stuckness." It includes seven practices that will help you develop the inner strength to confront what holds you back in life and prevents you from creating a life you love living. You will feel empowered to liberate yourself from what keeps you stuck so you can take action and soar free. You will be free to Fly High.

The Fly-High Method is far from the typical self-help material in many ways.

It's an inside-out approach. When it comes to personal transformation, the way to ensure sustainable change is to be willing to go deep within yourself in order to discover and build on the foundational aspects of who you are at your core. You need to be open to finding out what you really need to be happy; how you feel about yourself; how you engage with those around you; and what you believe in and stand for.

This method focuses on changing your life from the inside out. Each practice takes you within, so you can focus on a singular, internal aspect of who you are at your core—your beliefs, feelings, thoughts, spirit, inner child, and even your relationships. Each practice can set in motion a systemic shift in how you feel, think, and behave. Once you are in a good place inside, a chain reaction will take place and all the external aspects of your life will come together smoothly and effortlessly.

If your heart is full and smiling, your relationships will be positive, your work will feel fulfilling. And, overall, your life will feel meaningful.

Each practice instills hope and possibility. It's our natural tendency to avoid the unknown and fall back on the "known," even when what we know it is not healthy for us. Our willingness to fix what is keeping us stuck will kickstart when we regain hope for a better tomorrow—we are able to visualize new possibilities, and we feel empowered to act.

To inspire you to take positive action, each practice in the Fly-High Method follows a three-part approach that includes powerful storytelling, pragmatic advice, and healing activities.

Each of the Fly-High practices begins with raw, personal storytelling that illustrates how I turned what hurt the most into jet fuel to transform my life—from a place of want and failure to a place of fulfillment and triumph. I will give you a front-row seat to the epiphanies that came to me after making monumental mistakes, finding myself in the thick of experiences that knocked me on my butt many times, and enduring epic failures that had me crying all night.

Because if I can create a wonderful life despite what I have lived, so can you.

The second phase offers pragmatic tried-and-tested perspectives, and advice that leverages my professional expertise, personal experience, and the blessings from experts in psychology, life coaching, relationship management, and metaphysics—all bundled and delivered with love and affection. It's the type of advice and life-changing wisdom that you would get if someone who loved you dearly and had a Ph.D. in life's "school of hard knocks" took you under their wing and shared with you the secrets that turned their life around.

And, finally, each practice concludes with exercises created to inspire and relax you. The aim is to leave you feeling hopeful about the future, full of positive energy and feeling like anything is possible. In this nurturing and grounded space, you can focus on aspects within yourself that are often scattered. Here, you can feel relaxed and calm, and compelled to care and look after yourself.

This three-phase approach will open your mind to possibilities you never considered—and will have you feeling optimistic and hopeful about your future.

This approach accelerates your pace of change. The order of the practices is naturally conducive to *behavior stacking*— they are intentionally organized to optimize your level of self-discovery, healing, and positive change. This sequencing takes you through the seven practices in a way that maximizes their impact—so you see transformative results not only in one segment of your life but across all your internal layers— relatively quickly.

"'Behavior-stacking' accelerates transformation in every segment of your life. Each of the seven practices build upon each other."

For example, the first practice helps you shed false core beliefs about yourself that hold you back from making transformative changes. Once you give yourself license to let go of these beliefs and decide to respectfully disregard them, you are ready to take on practice number two, which shows you a new way to live your life that is based on what gives your life meaning. The third practice comes in to help you tame the negative self-talk that can prevent you from making the first two practices part of your day-to-day experience. All practices stack on top of each other and build on one another to help you see positive changes quickly.

The Fly-High Method combines practicality with a touch of magic. Most powerful shifts happen during an altered state of consciousness—when you are able to transcend the physical and connect with what's inside of you.

Toward that goal, each of the practices provides not only advice and perspective on "what" could be different, but also shows you "how" to incorporate it into your unique life circumstances. Through powerful visualization exercises, you are transported to magical places, surrounded by beauty and compassion.

Here, safe and nurtured, you can take refuge from your current reality and instead take the time to go deep inside yourself. You'll remember, wonder, and contemplate. You'll feel entertained, hopeful, and inspired. In this place of magic, you become aware of important information that will help you make informed decisions that lead to powerful changes.

You'll reconnect with what you stand for. You will know how to use your personal power to touch the lives of others in a positive way. You will know what to do to ensure that other people are uplifted simply by being in your presence. You will feel compelled to be a force for good, to commit to helping others, to make this world a better place. You will learn how wonderful it can feel when you help others to soar to higher ground.

Plus, it's fun! Some people avoid doing inner work because they think it will be scary, messy, and lonely. But with the assistance of seven nurturing cows as your guides, the process of going deep within yourself to reconnect with your inner essence can be enjoyable and fun.

You will benefit from the loving energy of these animals who embody the attributes they symbolize: Patience, calm, nourishment, abundance, fertility, potential, possibility, and grounding.

Each cow will guide you through an exercise where you will reconnect with those parts of you that make you unique, beautiful, and extraordinary. This enriching process of finding out about yourself is energizing, playful—fun.

You will fall in love with your guides. But, most importantly, you will fall in love with yourself.

Commit to Adding These Practices to Your Day-to-Day

Ultimately, the Fly-High Method will expand your perspective about how you see yourself and how you fit into the world around you. With a daily commitment to the mindsets, heart-sets, and rituals outlined within the seven practices, you will have the inner strength to help yourself get unstuck from whatever situation you find yourself in.

When you make the seven practices part of your day-to-day, you will learn to:

- **Challenge the external models of dos and don'ts.** You'll be inspired to shed those external layers that keep you stuck and enslaved to old paradigms, outdated rulebooks, and limiting conventions.

- **Hear what your heart has been trying to tell you for a long time.** When was the last time you listened—*really* listened—to what your heart was asking for? You will find out how wonderful it feels to finally understand what your heart needs to feel full and satisfied and why it is important to pause and listen to yourself before reacting to external stimuli.

- **Identify and silence the "committee" inside your head**. That annoying mental chatter that keeps reminding you of all those "should," "musts," and "oughts" needs to go. You will learn how to yank the plug on this committee and stop it from taking charge of your well-being, your much-needed sleep, and your decision-making.

- **Surround yourself only with people who enliven and encourage you.** By doing this, you become your best possible self. You will look at the people in your life with a clear, nonjudgmental, loving gaze and discern who you need to let go of and who you want to invite even closer.

- **Reconnect with your inner essence.** Your essence is that part of you who knows what is truly best for you, who sees things through a higher and broader lens, opening your eyes to new possibilities. By tapping into it for inspiration and creativity, you will come to trust your intuition that points the way when clouds dim your light.

- **Have fun again!** You will be able to kick back your heels, relax, and truly *enjoy* life. You will know how to face challenges with the optimistic viewpoint of a child and how to rekindle the relationship with that playful child inside you, so you can see life as a playground full of opportunities and adventures.

The Fly-High Method guidance and exercises can be done again and again, each time helping you to soar higher and discover more and more about your inner self and what makes you truly happy. You will want to come back to it on a regular basis for perspective, inspiration, motivation, or just a boost of positive energy. The possibilities are endless.

The important thing is to be intentional about these practices and to be open to whatever comes to you with your cow's loving guidance.

I hope you'll be as amazed as I was—and that you'll soar as high as you can dream!

3

The Seven Daring Practices of the Fly-High Method

Flip Your Focus Inward and Challenge
External Models of Dos and Don'ts

Listen to Your Heart—It's Hungry for Attention!

Yank the Plug on the "Itty-Bitty-Shitty Committee"

Honor the Light Within Yourself

Inspire Your Inner Child to Come Out and Play

Grow High-Caliber Relationships—They Matter!

Help Others Soar Higher

Practice #1:

Flip Your Focus Inward and Challenge External Models of Dos and Don'ts

My Life Skyrocketed When I Challenged the Rules I Lived By

When I was six, I was given a blonde doll with big blue eyes that opened and closed. Her name was Magdalena, and I instantly fell in love with her.

Just as I was eagerly about to get her out of the box and hug her, my mother stopped me. I was not allowed to take her out of the box because she would get dirty. For a long time, I spent every free moment staring at Magdalena through the clear plastic. I would move the box vertically and horizontally so that she would open and close her eyes, and I would sit there mesmerized by her long eyelashes and beautiful blue eyes.

Wanting things that I couldn't have made me even more hungry for what money could buy. In addition, when eventually I arrived in the United States at the age of twelve, I experienced firsthand society's cold shoulder, which further fed my intense desire to achieve. I never wanted to feel the sharp blade of humiliation again, that feeling that cut right through my insides when others made me feel inferior because I didn't speak English, didn't have money, didn't fit in.

I became obsessed with what society valued, and I was willing to work extremely hard to achieve whatever that was. I became so driven in my quest that I finished college in less than three years, earning a degree in accounting, a field I didn't know anything about aside from that it paid well.

And even though I quickly learned that I was not wired to be an accountant, I dismissed the disappointment I felt inwardly and hunkered down, determined to be successful in the world of finance.

I become so influenced by external factors that I relentlessly chased after things I believed were essential to my happiness.

I worked hard for a higher performance rating at work, earning the next rungs up the corporate ladder, a bigger house, a flashy car, the best school for my children, and the trendiest clothes—right down to the brand of my purse.

What I didn't realize at the time is that I had lost connection with my true self. Influenced so strongly by external factors and experiences, I didn't even know anymore what made me *me*. What did I really value? What were my passions? What special talents had I been blessed with? I didn't have a clue.

> *"I was a huge success—at*
> *meeting others' expectations.*
> *But I needed to work on knowing*
> *what I expected of myself."*

I was so disconnected from the *real me,* that it took a personal tragedy to reset my perspective about what's important in life.

My husband and I lived in New Jersey where a community of fellow Spaniards had settled. We'd all known each other for years—everyone had a strong opinion about each other's lives, and gossip was the norm. Just months before my husband and I were to divorce he took his own life.

Before his death, we had to endure becoming the center of the town's rumor mill over our divorce. After his death, I had to face it alone. And it just got worse.

What followed was the darkest period of my life. Not only did I lose my husband, a man I was married to for 23 years, but the close community I'd grown up in turned on me as well. According to them, it was my fault he'd died because I had asked for a divorce.

With only my children and a handful of friends to lean on, I felt bereft, alone, and betrayed. I hurt in ways that I didn't know were possible. Tears were my steady companion, to the point that most of my eyelashes fell out from so much crying.

It took a while and many ghastly encounters with people who hurt me deeply to eventually conclude that *I had to flip my perspective inward*. I had to stop living my life based on those external models of dos and don'ts.

When I finally realized that I could challenge all my belief systems. All the stuff in my head that was informing my decisions could be questioned and disputed, all the programming that had me doing things because others said so, or thought so, could be rewritten and even purged. That was when my life began to shift.

When I gave myself license to challenge all the "rulebooks," even the ones my family passed down to me, when I gave myself the freedom to reexamine what had been inculcated in my head about what is important, when I dared to abandon what the media and society had brainwashed me about what I could do, should do, and even what I should look like—when I gave myself permission to dismiss public opinion, I became liberated from shackles that had enslaved me.

I freed myself from a way of life that was suffocating and painful.

What followed surprised me. Instead of the world outside dictating what I did, I started setting the tone for the world around me. I went from a place of weakness (despite all I had acquired along the way), feeling belittled and insignificant, to a place of strength. My self-confidence skyrocketed. I not only survived my husband's suicide—a tragedy that could have destroyed me, our family, and my friendships. But my children and I achieved what others thought impossible: we created a dream life for ourselves in which we are now soaring high, personally and professionally.

This new perspective made me feel like that little girl who was not allowed to remove her doll from the box, who had been told that she could not play with it because it was for display purposes only, was finally ripping through the box and the plastic, tearing down the barriers that stood between me and a fulfilling life.

We Can All Learn to (Respectfully) Disregard Most External Models of Dos and Don'ts

When we feel stuck, it's vital to pay close attention to our inner world. Are we being true to who we are inside? Most of us hide what is real and authentic about ourselves because we don't feel safe showing the outside world who we truly are. We are afraid to let others have access to those parts of us that are most vulnerable, those parts deep inside that are most precious to us.

What we don't realize is that when we hide who we truly are, we run the risk of living our lives based on how the world around us says we should. We run the risk of following external models of dos and don'ts that are not necessarily aligned with our own values, standards, passions, and our gifts and talents. We run the risk of missing opportunities to live in integrity with our own inner beings and instead going through life feeling unfulfilled.

For instance, what happens if our internal wiring is naturally creative and artistic, if we see ourselves dancing on a stage or playing an instrument with a rock band or at the symphony, but we grew up in a family that looks down on the arts? They may have been grooming us since childhood for a profession that they thought was best for us—even though our true nature reflects something else.

If we don't stand up for our calling and our own passions, we run the risk of being miserable for the rest of our lives doing something we dread.

What if we are surrounded by people who have very strict belief systems about gender identity and sexual orientation, but who we are inside clashes and breaks through all those belief systems?

We will be living a lie, feeling angry and afraid until we allow *the real us* to come out.

We might live surrounded by pressure to be rich and powerful, to own the big mansion and the fast car; to be famous and successful; to have thousands of people liking our posts on social media. But deep inside, what if we really crave a quiet life and being of service to others?

Until we live in integrity with who we are inside, we will feel empty and dissatisfied, no matter how many things we surround ourselves with.

Think about it...

- How can we enjoy what we do for a living if we're not being true to our talents and gifts?

- How can we be successful and stand out if we lose our uniqueness by trying to fit in?

- How can we rise for a higher cause when we don't know what we stand for?

- How can we truly appreciate the person in the mirror if we allow society to dictate what is beautiful or special?

Finding the Courage to Be True to Ourselves

It takes courage to tell our loved ones we are taking a different path in life than the one they charted for us, to go against the grain of what the rest of the world thinks is right, to challenge the system and existing norms; to voice our opinion when we know it will be frowned upon, to show our true colors and risk being disliked or judged.

It's not always easy to be real, but the alternative is far more painful. When we are not true to our values, talents and passions, our moral compass, our history, heritage, and ethnicity—to all the attributes that define us at our core and make us real—our foundation is weak. And our foundation is what holds everything else together.

When our foundation is not right, we will struggle in all other aspects of our lives: in our relationships, our jobs, in our social connections—in fact, everywhere.

If we are confused about who we are inside, the other areas of our lives will be messy, too.

We owe it to ourselves to find out who we really are inside, what we stand for, what we believe in, what we are willing to fight for, and to learn what makes us tick.

Once we know what all that is, we owe it to ourselves to put all the external models of dos and don'ts we have been abiding by to the test, to determine if they encourage or deter us from living our lives from a place of authenticity.

The easiest way to assess if an external model is right for us is by asking ourselves these questions:

- Does this model encourage my individuality, independence, and autonomy?

- Do these rules and paradigms bring out the best in me?

- Do I feel good about myself and my life when I adhere to this way of thinking?

- Does it honor my innermost being?

As we go through this assessment, we will notice that some of our answers truly resonate with who we are at our core. Others will need to be (respectfully) disregarded.

Freeing ourselves from the burden of caring about external models does not mean that we don't care about other people or that we are self-centered. It means that we no longer blindly accept traditions, conventions, trends, and public opinion. We consciously ensure our choices are in our highest interest and that they are free from influences that are not in integrity with what makes us happy.

It means we give ourselves license to look at the spectrum of choices and decide what truly suits us. For example, if the standard relationship models don't support our circumstances and hold us back from doing what truly makes us feel happy, we need to give ourselves the freedom to figure out what relationship model is right for us and then put it in place, without regard for what others think is right or wrong. Tradition is wonderful, but if it holds us back from being true to who we are, we ought to respectfully disregard it.

The same applies to the way we raise our children. If they have unique needs or if our circumstances are not typical, we don't have to blindly adhere to traditional models of education just because other people do.

We owe it to our children and to ourselves to research options and then put in place what will bring out the best in our children.

The same applies to models for making a living, for overall wellness, for definitions of beauty, for how we practice spirituality. For everything.

Our Rebels Have an Important Cause

The point here is not to just go against the system because we can. This is not about being a rebel without a cause. We need to find the courage to push back on those models that hold us back from living our lives from a place of authenticity.

Because if we don't stand up for the real person within, who will?

Imagine if we flipped our perspective inward, if we took away the power the outside world has over us, and instead looked for our own internal definition of who we are and what we are worth. Imagine if we set our own standards for what we value, what we believe in, what we stand for, and what makes our hearts and souls happy.

Imagine living a life in which we…

- Are comfortable in our own skin, regardless of age, skin color, ethnicity, size, sexual orientation, or other external classifications.

- Make decisions while trusting our internal systems and would march to our own unconventional beat, not caring what others have to say.

- Subscribe to the belief that spirituality is not inherited, it's discovered.

- Are self-fulfilled and don't need to rely on others to make us happy because we know that true happiness comes from within.

- Own our story—warts and all—and recognize that we are works in progress.

- Live our lives from a place where we are in integrity with our hearts and souls.

We would have the freedom to let the most beautiful version of ourselves come through—our natural self, unaltered. We would soar free from old tapes that are no longer relevant, beliefs that don't serve our best interests, other people's influences that hijack our perspective, and imprints that clutter our judgment with false impressions of what is important and needed.

We can give ourselves permission to become unstuck from what is holding us back from being real and true to ourselves.

When we lovingly embrace who we really are, the part deep within that is true and beautiful, we empower ourselves to direct our lives in the direction that truly feeds our hearts and souls.

Directed Visualization #1

The Flying Cows Dare You to Embrace the Real You

The flying cows gave themselves permission to be true to their inner selves and achieve what seemed impossible—to fly!

IMAGINE YOURSELF WALKING ALONG *a country lane toward a beautiful green meadow. The stress of the world around you has you feeling a bit rattled and scattered and you are looking to unwind and reground yourself. It's a warm, sunny day. The sun shines brightly from a deep blue sky, and its warmth enfolds your body.*

You notice a sunny spot in the meadow right next to a patch of lavender and lie down comfortably on the soft, springy grass. As you breathe in the relaxing scent of lavender, your body begins to take in the soothing calmness of this beautiful place.

You gaze up at the deep blue sky and the fluffy white clouds that look like gigantic cotton balls. Birds are singing in the pine trees nearby.

Then from the corner of your eye, you see seven cows, jumping from cloud to cloud. They are kicking their heels up to the heavens, mooing in delight.

You smile at such a sight, knowing that you are beyond the realm of time or space, in a place where anything is possible. You breathe in and then let out a deep sigh of relief, of happiness, knowing that here you are, free to be your true self. Here, you can let your guard down. You can shed the old crusty layers of protection that you have wrapped around yourself. Here, you are completely safe.

Pinta, the biggest and most matronly of the seven cows, floats gently down to come close by your side. She is massive, gentle, and loving. And her calmness soothes and comforts.

WITHOUT ANY APPREHENSION, you go to her and begin to rub her thick black and white coat. You gaze into her tender eyes. You know that she is there to help you reconnect with your authentic self. To reconnect to the part of you that is genuine and true.

She begins by asking you to recall every role you play: parent, child, sibling, partner, lover, student, teacher. As each role comes into your mind, Pinta asks you to let it go.

She asks you to imagine yourself letting go of these titles and labels.

Then she asks you to visualize yourself letting go of everything you own: your car, house, furniture, clothes, money in the bank, toys, even your shoes.

And then, just when you think there isn't any more to let go of, she asks you to see yourself without everything external to you that you cherish most in the world: your family, your friends, your community, your heritage, even your beliefs.

As all the outer layers fluff off and your inner being begins to come through, you start to feel a little vulnerable and exposed. Then you see your reflection in Pinta's eyes. You see the most perfect version of yourself. You are amazed at how lovable and endearing you really are.

You are beautiful. Pure.

Now Pinta asks you to reflect on what this wonderful version of you values most of all. What motivates you? Is it loyalty, altruism, power, security, tradition? What informs your ideals and principles?

Who are you, deep inside?

Once you have identified what the truest version of you values, look at yourself once again in Pinta's eyes. Now, see all the things that make you unique: your gifts and talents, your exceptional abilities, your kindness, your passions, your longings—all the things that make you you.

Pinta then asks you to look even deeper: What inspires you? What makes you tick? What do you stand for? What are you willing to die for?

ONCE YOU TRULY FEEL the many attributes that shape who you are inside, again gaze deeply into Pinta's eyes, feel her soft warm breath on you, and wrap your arms around yourself. Give yourself a big hug. Embrace the real you.

With her loving eyes, Pinta reassures you that your authentic self is uniquely perfect, lovable, and worthy. She encourages *you to accept, nurture, and encourage this beautiful part of you so it can grow and blossom.*

It can now set the tone for a lifestyle where who you are inside shines through—and makes you glow on the outside. It shines in your relationships, work, and hobbies. It shines in all areas of your life.

Before Pinta rejoins her pals up in the sky, she reminds you that every time the outside world has you wanting to hide the real you, you can come back to the meadow and be with her. She is always there to help you reconnect with your authentic self.

As Pinta waves goodbye, she dares you one last time to embrace the real you. Because when you do, you put your best foot forward, and you position yourself to achieve anything your heart desires.

...Even something that the outside world might consider impossible.

Practice #2:

Listen to Your Heart.

It's Hungry for Attention!

My Heart Was Starved for Meaning

A lot has happened since those days when I worked and played with the cows in my hometown in northern Spain. Looking back, I am amazed at how I could live in such a state of joy when I had so little. We shared our home with the animals and all that came with them—including the rancid smell of manure and the hundreds of annoying flies.

When I was five, my dad brought home a small television set that he had bought secondhand. (I was more amused by the antenna looking like rabbit ears than by the set itself.)

That television changed the energy of our small town. Even though the black and white screen was small and fuzzy, every Sunday at four in the afternoon, our town's three families gathered in our small kitchen to watch a series about a horse called *Furia*. We would all sit in silence as if we were at church, and as soon as it was over, we would talk over each other about what Furia had done. As I recall those days, I can't help but smile. My heart had all it needed to feel full.

As the years went by and painful experiences came my way, I lost connection with what it needed to feel as full as it once did. Instead, I focused my energy on building an impressive resumé and materially supporting a successful family. I hoped all the professional achievements I attained would give me that sense of deeper fulfillment I once had.

What I felt instead was a constant hunger that couldn't be satisfied. The temporary gratifications that came from a highly coveted assignment or the job-well-done recognitions and promotions were closely followed by feelings of stagnation. Soon, I would begin to crave the next thing that I believed would fill the emptiness I felt inside.

Everyone experiences this emptiness differently and tries to fill it in their own way. In my case, I kept chasing more responsibility, bigger projects, more impressive titles, and more money—often at the expense of my well-being. Ambition became an addiction that kept me constantly craving a fix at any cost. This lifestyle ultimately led me to a place where my health took a scary nosedive. I knew, deep inside, that I was going to die young if I didn't find a different path.

Seeking a better direction, I began exploring ways to align what I did for a living with my life purpose. All the experts said that I would feel happier, more fulfilled, if I aligned how I was living with my life purpose. It all sounded great, but there was a problem: besides raising my son and daughter to be happy and productive adults, I had no clue what my purpose in life was.

As I continued the search, I wasn't any clearer about my own purpose, and was starting to question the endeavor itself. I was infuriated by the truth that most people on the planet live in dire poverty. If they were just to align themselves to their life purpose, would everything be fine for them?

How does the belief in a "life purpose" help the mother of five who must walk six hours every day just to haul water for her family? How does it enlighten the farmer who is experiencing severe drought and his family is starving? How does it serve anyone who is suffering from loss, hardship, and hopelessness?

And aside from all that, what does it *really* mean to follow your life purpose?

These questions swirled around and around in my mind and eventually led me to sign up for a retreat that would eventually change the way I approach life from then on.

This Was No Retreat—it Was More Like a Nudge Forward

During the retreat, I was introduced to the idea that everyone's life purpose comes down to feeling satisfied inside. And that internal satisfaction is not found in "doing," but is found instead in "feeling." Happiness is not attained by what we have or what we do, but by how we feel about what we have and do.

The teachings at this retreat helped me see that my heart has its own unique set of needs that it had been craving since I was a child. If I didn't make important changes, my heart would continue to feel famished and would seek contentment in external forms of appeasement, such as in relationships, careers, food, or even drugs and alcohol. On the other hand, if I gently fed my heart with what it truly craved, then it would feel full and satisfied.

This approach intrigued me and resonated with me. But, besides those wonderful memories of being happy with my cows, *I had no idea what my heart was hungry for*.

With anticipation and a touch of apprehension, I set out to take a dive into what my heart craves most. The goal was to identify my heart's core needs. Basically, I had to figure out the top four or five needs that trigger the deepest reactions and that pull my heartstrings the most.

During this enlightening retreat, I was instructed to begin my dive by revisiting the happiest and saddest moments from my childhood.

Then I had to identify which core need was being met, or not, during those moments.

The third, and final, step was to determine whether that need has played a key role in my life.

I was able to identify one of my core needs by recalling a happy memory of playing in the mud. While the cows were peacefully grazing, I would mix dry grass with mud, and then mold and shape it into rectangles and triangles that looked like little pyramids. I'd also create little statues of people and animals, which I would then put out in the sun to dry. The end product was my own organic version of Legos. I'd use the dry mud pieces to build large castles.

I would allow my imagination to run free, making believe I was a loving and generous queen who looked after everyone in her kingdom.

I had loved those moments because I was able to build something beautiful out of nothing. This was much bigger than having the freedom to be creative—it was about finding exceptional solutions to seemingly unsolvable problems. By being ingenious and tapping into my imagination, I was able to fill a need that I had as a child: to have toys and playmates in my world. During those moments, though I didn't have the words yet to describe it, I felt brilliantly creative.

I started thinking about other times throughout my life when I had this need. At work, I loved coming up with creative ideas or solutions, and starting new groups and organizations; I loved, essentially, creating something valuable from nothing.

On a personal level, helping family, friends, and mentees come up with resourceful solutions to their thorniest of problems has always been deeply gratifying.

Conversely, by going back to some of my saddest times, I was able to identify another one of my core needs. When I was abruptly left behind at the convent, I lost everything I had had a connection with up till then. I was even stripped of my name and was instead referred to as "number four." During those dreadful years with the nuns, I felt as though I didn't matter at all. As an adult, reflecting on that pain, I realized that it's critical to my happiness to know that I *do* matter and that I *am* important.

I realized I feel my best when I'm recognized for who I truly am and the gifts I bring to my relationships. When I'm acknowledged and appreciated, I experience a profound sense of fulfillment. At work, when what I produce has an impact on others and on the world, I feel empowered and satisfied.

The Epiphanies Were Life-Changing

During my retreat, I decoded five core needs that make my heart sing with joy:

- Being creative

- Feeling important and that I matter

- Being my true self

- Making a difference in the lives of those I love and in the world around me

- Unconditional love and acceptance of those who matter to me

The moment I saw this list unfold in front of me, I started to cry. I finally understood why I had been so happy with so little as a child, and why, even though I had so much as an adult, I felt so miserable and empty. As a child, the little creative problem-solver inside me had total freedom to come out and play. I felt that I mattered and that what I did every day was important to my family and to the cows.

I felt totally accepted for who I was.

No one ever judged me or tried to change me. My work made a difference, and I felt an unconditional bond with all the people I loved and with my beloved cows. While in the midst of poverty, this little girl was getting her heart fed with everything she needed to feel happy.

As an adult, living a lavish lifestyle, I was walking around with a heart that was starving to death. The creative problem-solver in me felt stifled. I didn't feel like I mattered or was appreciated at all. In fact, totally the opposite: I was feeling used and taken advantage of. I lived in constant fear of disapproval and judgment.

While I had a big title, I didn't feel what I did for a living was important or that I was making a difference. Although I adored my children, and they provided me an experience of unconditional love, it wasn't enough.

No wonder I was so unhappy.

As I sat there, with tears rolling down my face, I had one of the biggest epiphanies of my life. I finally understood why I felt so empty, and why everything I had tried up till then hadn't worked. I had been trying to fill my heart by accomplishing goals, rather than feeding it the experiences it was starving for.

The Secret to a Meaningful Life
Is Found Within Our Hearts

When we feel stuck in life, some of us seek ways out by asking ourselves questions such as, "Why am I here?" and "What is my purpose in life?" Some of us have clear and automatic responses to these. But for many of us, the answers to those questions are hard to come by and the possibilities are too abstract and nebulous.

"If our hearts are full,
our lives will have meaning;
we will have purpose."

Plus, this assumes that "life purpose" relates only to what we do for a living. What happens when the best thing for our family is for us to be a stay-at-home parent? Does this mean we are not living our purpose? What about the mother in Africa that must walk hours every day to haul water for her family? Is that her purpose?

Living our purpose comes down to living our lives in a way that ensures fulfillment. Fulfillment is not determined by how much we own, what we do for a living, what roles we play, what titles we have, how many people know us, or who we have by our side. Our degree of fulfillment is determined by how full or empty our hearts are. If our hearts are being fed on a regular basis, we will feel fulfilled in life—even if we live a very modest and simple lifestyle.

But if our hearts are running on empty, we will feel dissatisfied regardless of all the amazing things we surround ourselves with.

If that mother in Africa has a happy heart, her life may feel a lot more fulfilling and purposeful than an executive in a well air-conditioned office who has no heart connection to his or her work.

Regardless of our external circumstances, if our hearts are full, our lives will have meaning to us; we will have purpose.

So, if the chain reaction that leads us to living lives that feel meaningful begins with making sure our hearts are full, what do we need to feed them?

The answer is different for each of us. Our hearts are all wired differently and what our hearts value most is unique to each of us.

Finding out what our hearts crave is of utmost importance— it's the recipe to our joy and happiness, to lives that feel fulfilling and meaningful.

Once we discover what our hearts value most, it becomes the "success criteria" for our decisions and choices. This list will help us make better, more informed decisions about what jobs will feel more gratifying, which romantic interests will be best for our well-being, what hobbies will feel more nourishing to who we are inside, and what lifestyles will bring us the most satisfaction.

Here's How It Works...

Imagine your heart places the most value on adventure, belonging, being appreciated, and being needed in an almost hero-like way. If you set a goal to find a job that can satisfy that need daily, you won't search for a job that would have you spending your day at a desk. Instead, you would set an objective to end up in a high-energy, thrill-seeking, hands-on job that is different every day and is of service to others.

And when you land that job, it will not feel like a job, it will feel more like a calling—because that's what it is.

Now imagine if what your heart values the most is unbounded creative expression, feeling as though you matter, being authentic and real, and making a difference. If you used these needs as the measuring tape for finding a great relationship, you would set an intention for finding someone who makes you feel accepted and loved just the way you are. You'll want to know you are a priority.

Perhaps you want your partner to share your need to make a difference in the world, or at least support you in your dream to do so. Your heart will feel happy with someone who encourages your creativity and your unconventional perspectives. And when you find a connection like this, it will feel like you have found your soulmate—because you have.

If your heart puts a high value on having a deep spiritual connection, contributing to the lives of others—and you need to feel valued, indispensable, and admired—you will make your decisions based on what your heart wants. If you use this list to make decisions about what to do with your free time, chances are that taking art classes at the local school isn't going to energize you. But if you find a hobby that is closely associated with a spiritual community, for example, where you can play a key role in which you receive recognition for the impact your efforts have on others, you will be a very happy camper.

All Aspects of Our Lives Should Feed Our Hearts

The is no right or wrong when it comes to the heart. There is no place for judgment when trying to identify what it needs. It wants what it wants, as the saying goes. Each of us is different. And, while how we express and manifest what we need might change as we mature and evolve in our lives, what the heart values most—the things it is truly hungry for—does not change. If our heart places a high value on feeling secure and safe, it will crave that throughout life and that core need will arise in the decisions we make, consciously or subconsciously.

We owe it to ourselves to find what our heart is hungry for and proactively feed it in constructive and positive ways.

Ideally, we want to work toward the goal of having all aspects of our lives feed our hearts, but if we find ourselves in circumstances where this isn't feasible, we owe it to ourselves to at least strive to have some areas of our lives that do.

For example, if you find yourself in an unfulfilling job that doesn't feed your heart, but you need the job to pay the rent and put food on the table, you will have to find other ways to feed your heart, whether that's through hobbies, relationships, or other experiences. Otherwise, you run the risk of falling into a place of hopelessness and despair—and all the toxicity that comes with those dark emotions.

For our lives to feel meaningful, our hearts must be constantly fed in some sort of way.

Making a practice to constantly strategize how to feed our hearts is a foundational step to getting unstuck and creating a wonderful life. But this can be taken one step further.

This practice has a broader application: it can be extremely valuable in our relationships. Imagine if we not only knew what we needed but we also knew what the people in our lives craved deep inside. We would have the blueprint to healthy and happy relationships.

Imagine how life-altering a conversation with our children would be if, instead of asking them, "What do you want to do when you grow up?" we asked, "What does your heart crave?" Then, we could help them figure out how to build stable and grounded lives that are simultaneously fulfilling and meaningful, while allowing them to feel every day what they crave the most inside. There would probably be a lot fewer people paying off student loans for degrees they regret pursuing.

Imagine if we knew what our partners needed to feel fulfilled? We would have the recipe for stronger bonds and deeper connections. If we know that being appreciated is one of their core needs, we could honor what their heart values most by letting them know, on a regular basis, how much we appreciate them. It would also help avoid the tripwires that trigger arguments. When someone who values being appreciated feels unappreciated, the hurt feels way more pungent than to someone who doesn't have this core need. Knowing what our partner's heart craves—and being able to nourish that—gives us the foundation for relationships that can stay strong no matter what storms come our way.

Creating lives in which we live this way will not happen overnight, especially if we are starting from places of total turmoil. But, by setting the intention to make decisions going forward that are in integrity with what our hearts and the hearts of those we care deeply about, our lives will begin to make traction in the right direction.

We are all unique and we all have different needs. We owe it to ourselves to find out what our hearts are hungry for and to make conscious decisions to feed them regularly. When we do, our lives will feel more meaningful and purposeful, and we will live from a place of joy and fulfillment—regardless of our external circumstances.

Directed Visualization #2

The Flying Cows Dare You to Listen to Your Heart

The flying cows listened to their hearts and elevated their reality to extraordinary heights.

SEE YOURSELF WALKING *through a green meadow with pine trees all around. It's early morning and the sun is starting to come up.*

A warm breeze softly caresses your cheek. As you breathe in the fresh air you notice the smell of flowers coming from the large patch of wild daisies growing nearby. You smile inwardly, and the fragrance calms your mind.

As you look up, Mother Nature is painting a beautiful abstract in the sky: vibrant orange and purple mingle together and overlay a sea of blue. Streaks of gold from the morning sun peek through. You gaze up at the exquisite colors and images.

And then you notice something up there. The flying cows are frolicking, laughing, and mooing with delight! You chuckle out loud. You know you have entered a realm where the thinking mind is not in control, and it's perfectly okay.

Cora, one of the most loving of the cows, comes down to be by your side. You place your hand on her head to pet her soft caramel-colored coat. She has a small white spot on her forehead that mimics the shape of a heart. It makes you smile.

YOU FEEL COMPLETELY RELAXED *and at ease standing with Cora. You can sense her beautiful heart and quickly feel a connection with her, along with an innate sense of trust.*

Cora shares with you that she is here to help you connect with your heart.

What will make your heart feel full and satisfied? She is here to help you find out.

As you look into Cora's warm brown eyes, you see yourself as a small child, playing your favorite game of make-believe. Those times were so magical, you could spend hours and hours playing it. Cora asks you to go back in time and to name the feelings that made those moments feel so wonderful.

Cora murmurs to you, "Go deeper than just the surface feelings. Yes, happy. Yes, contented. But what else?"

She nudges you to go deeper and deeper until you pinpoint the feelings that in the past truly resonated with your heart and made it hum.

You're looking for what touched your internal cords, the experience of feeling unique, extraordinary, admired, powerful, loved, nurtured, important, or needed.

Cora reminds you that there is no right or wrong. She asks you not to place judgment on what bubbles up, and to not allow your mind to get in the way. This is what your heart has to say—so just let it come up.

ONCE YOU GET CLEAR *on your heart's most vital need, Cora encourages you to keep looking until you have at least four or five on your list and reminds you that the effort will be well worth it.*

She also reminds you that sometimes your core needs are found in the most painful experiences. By gazing into her warm brown eyes, you know that it's okay to travel back in time to a place when your heart hurt deeply, perhaps to a situation that jabbed your heart in ways you didn't think you would survive.

As you feel Cora's breath by your side, you are reassured that you are not alone, that you are safe, and that you are loved.

Now you find the courage to go back to a chapter in your life where your heart truly ached. When you begin to feel anxious and nervous, Cora lovingly suggests that you ask your hurting heart to tell you what it was starving for during that time. What did it need so badly that it wasn't getting?

AS YOUR HEART OPENS, *Cora shares with you that knowledge is power. Knowing what is important to your heart will put you in a place of authority, so you can take command of your circumstances. Never again will you settle for a life in which your heart is not full and happy. You feel empowered by this.*

Once you feel you have discovered those things that your heart values the most, Cora lets you know that this is a life-

changing moment; one worthy of celebration. You have just uncovered the key to your own heart, the key that unlocks the door to a great life, one in which you use these needs as the basis for almost all your decisions. In this new life, your heart plays a primary role, and you make choices by considering what your heart needs.

Before Cora prepares to rejoin her friends up in the sky, she tells you that every time you lose sight of what gives you meaning and purpose, you can come back to the meadow and be with her. She is always there to help you reconnect with your heart.

As she waves goodbye, she reminds you that your purpose in life is to create a life you love living. And that the best way to do this is to listen to what your heart craves, to allow it to point the way, to trust that it knows best—because it does!

Practice #3:

*Y*ank the Plug on the "Itty-Bitty-Shitty Committee"

My Mental Rants Have Been My Most Ruthless Adversary

When I was small, the people in my little town in Spain wore *chancas*, homemade footwear resembling heavy construction boots and made from wood, cowhide, and tack nails. The wood soles were hand carved according to foot size, the hide was cut into a pattern that when stitched together would mold around the foot, and then both were nailed together with tack nails. Strings of leather were used as laces and tack nails were added to the bottom for traction so we wouldn't slip and slide.

Chancas were popular because they were cheap. But they were heavy, uncomfortable, often painful. And distractingly noisy. The irritating *tack-tack* sound of the nails hitting the stone pavement when people walked could be heard from quite a distance. I would make it a game to try to quiet my *chancas* but I failed at it every time. No matter what I did, the *chancas* would always win.

As life went on, I realized that my negative self-talk had a lot in common with my *chancas*. It was painfully uncomfortable, distractingly noisy, and hard to quiet.

As the years went by, my untamed negative talk took on a life of its own and grew into full-blown rants. The rants inside my head have been the most ruthless adversaries I have ever encountered. They have beaten me down when I was already on my knees. They have paralyzed me when I needed to jump. They have propelled me into the abyss when I ought to have stayed put.

They have taunted me and played every version of emotional warfare possible. They have pushed me into the darkest corners of my psyche, showed me terrifying ghosts that weren't there, and locked me up in the dungeon of despair, where I spent many long nights crying.

That ranting part of my mind has the power to engulf me in every form of self-judgment. At times it has had me juggling multiple forms simultaneously—its most wicked triads being shame, unworthiness, and inadequacy. Some of its other favorites have been fear of failure, fear of being poor again, fear of getting my heart broken again, fear of something happening to my loved ones, and fear of not being enough.

"The Committee" Talks Too Much

The negative talk in my head has been my kryptonite. It has the potential to drain all my power, leaving me defenseless.

It does not mess around.

There was a time when it cost me a huge career opportunity. A position that could have propelled my career forward became available, but the rant in my head told me I didn't have the experience needed or the right connections, and that I wouldn't be a good fit for the job.

It basically said, "you're not good enough for this." And I made the mistake of listening to all my negative talk and didn't even attempt to go for it.

The person hired for the position was far less qualified than I, and had none of the connections that I had. All the things my rant had pestered me with were completely false. Some months later, the person who would have been my boss invited me to lunch. He wanted to pick my brain about where he was taking the organization and ask my advice. Halfway through our luncheon, he asked me why I hadn't thrown my hat in the ring for the job since—given my experience and background—I would have been perfect for it. I was at a loss for words. All I could muster was, "The 'itty-bitty-shitty committee' in my head didn't let me."

We both burst into laughter, but there was sadness in the moment, too, because we both knew exactly what I meant.

Everyone does.

The best thing about that luncheon was that afterward I began to refer to my mental rants as "the committee." That switch turned out to be very helpful. It allowed me to treat it as a third party, like a group of crazy roommates that lives in my head. I was able to shift the control it had over me and the way I handled it. Making it something separate from my true self gave me license to respond—and to challenge it.

At times, I'll curse at "the committee." At other times I just laugh.

By treating "the committee" as a third party, I'm able to separate the rational and irrational. If I notice that I'm limiting myself from doing something—or if I am obsessing about an issue—I ask myself, "Is this truly me, or is this the committee acting up?"

By looking at my mental rant as a third party, I can examine it and determine if what's coming up is something I can deal with on my own? Or do I need a hand from a trusted friend or the assistance of a professional to help me work through it? Asking for help is sometimes the best and easiest thing we can do for ourselves.

The best part of identifying "the committee" in your head is that it gives me freedom to say, "I've had enough of you, and I don't have to listen to your nonsense anymore."

> *"Try telling your "committee"*
> *to take a seat. It's time to shush*
> *the negative rants."*

"The itty-bitty-shitty committee" label has resonated with many other people around me and has become a regular part of our conversations. It's like an exasperating acquaintance we all have in common.

I'll hear comments like, "The committee was out of control last night," when a friend couldn't sleep because old tapes kept replaying in her head. Or, "The committee came to visit and had me working overtime," when someone obsesses over whether to ask for a raise, or if they should break up with a boyfriend.

It also gives me language that creates space for easier conversations with others. If I have been ruminating about something that someone said or did, I can introduce the topic for discussion as, "I might be overthinking this, but 'the committee' will not shut up, so can we talk through it?"

It also lightens up our conversations and softens those times when we want to give advice. We can say, "Are you sure that's not your 'committee' acting up?"

Even though isolating the unhealthy blather and rants in my head has been life-changing, my "committee" and I would still be wrestling all the time for peace and quiet inside my head— if I hadn't found a daily practice that works.

For years, I looked for ways to arm myself against "the committee," or to disband it. I tried many mindfulness approaches, such as meditation, breath-work, yoga, sound therapy, painting, reading, and journaling. All of them worked somewhat but didn't give me the results I needed.

"Brain-Dumping" Helps to Silence My Rants

What has worked the best for me is what I call "brain dumping."

Every day I take 10 to 15 minutes to speed type whatever pops into my head. I don't worry about grammar or spelling. I close my eyes and just type whatever comes out in whatever order. Sometimes what comes out is dark; other times it's pleasant and cheerful. Occasionally, I find myself remembering something from my childhood or things I have been meaning to do in my daily life and somehow never get to. When I'm done typing, I don't read what I wrote. I close my laptop and continue with my day.

"Brain dumping" has become one of the most effective tools for me to better understand what's going on inside my head. It has brought to my attention all sorts of issues. Some I can resolve on my own, others make good conversation topics with mentors and friends, while larger concerns require advice from a therapist or other professional.

"Brain dumping" is now as much a part of my daily routine as brushing my teeth. If I don't do it, I feel off.

If I had not done the work to understand the programming inside my head and figured out my own way to tame the crazy rants my "committee" engages in, I would still be living a life absent of clarity and happiness. Instead, "the committee" is now a part of my mind that I have learned to master. For the most part, I'm in charge of it, and rarely do I allow it to take over.

The result? My feelings and thoughts are in alignment and I can make decisions freely, confidently, wisely, and with joy. And that little girl in me feels like she has finally won the game to quiet her *chancas*.

Grooming the Inside of Our Heads

If we peeked inside our heads, chances are we would find a wide variety of things: a fond memory of a trip we took, perhaps a childhood pleasure, a good friend or two we like to spend time with, something we enjoyed doing yesterday, a party we're anticipating tomorrow.

We might also find old pains that haven't healed; unresolved conflicts; cultural and religious beliefs that box us in; thoughts that hold us back or push us to do things we don't want to do; unhealthy patterns we keep repeating; fears that creep up; addictions we have a hard time shaking; destructive ambitions and desires. The list is limitless.

It's messy in there! Add these things to all the distractions we have in our lives—and it can become incredibly chaotic.

What's inside of our heads affects the way we think, which affects the way we feel, which affects the way we behave and the choices we make. Our thoughts have a direct impact on how we go about our lives.

If negative thoughts go unacknowledged or unaddressed, they have the power to become detrimental to our happiness and well-being. Our thoughts can be the key reason why we are stuck in the first place. Or, why we are not able to free ourselves from what holds us back.

But our minds are also our greatest allies in clearing the debris and scrubbing our thoughts clear again. It's crucial that we dedicate time and focused effort to keeping our thoughts fresh and sparkling.

Inner Grooming Helps You Scrub Away the Negativity

We invest a lot of time grooming the outside of our heads—combing and styling our hair, stroking just the right cream over our faces, carefully applying makeup, shaving, plucking, massaging, rinsing.

But do we invest as much time grooming the inside of our heads as we do the outside? This is even more important.

We need to find ways to get rid of all the messy, stinky ("shitty?") stuff inside our heads, so we can make room for new concepts and perspectives. By undergoing a regular ritual of internal grooming, we'll be empowered to challenge what isn't working in our lives. We'll feel the license to question our outworn beliefs and traditions and even see our old tapes in a new way.

Inner grooming gives us the freedom to challenge ourselves by asking *why* we are thinking certain thoughts. Are they part of some old programming pushing us to think this way? Or could they be significant and helpful?

Create a New Committee—of Trusted Advisors

One of the ways to jumpstart the grooming of what's inside our heads is with the help of an expert. A professional therapist can help us untangle snarls in our thinking and show us how to do it ourselves.

Also, having trusted advisors is essential. Making sure the people in our lives challenge our thinking, encourage our adventures, and are willing to support us as we shed our old skins is very important.

It's up to us to take responsibility for our internal grooming. It's up to us to groom our thoughts and emotions every day. Everyone is different, so finding the right daily routine is a matter of experimenting until we discover something we can stick to that resonates with our own personal preferences. It could be painting, writing, or chanting. The commitment to grooming practices is well worth the time we put into it.

How We Talk to—and About—Ourselves

One thing to keep in mind as we experiment with grooming practices is to be on the lookout for how we talk about ourselves. Words matter. And how we talk to ourselves plays a key role in how we think, feel, and act.

Here are a few approaches I've found helpful to change my habits in this area:

- **Rewording.** When you become aware of recurring self-defeating statements or sentences that you say either in your head or out loud, write them down. Then, practice rewording. For example, if you notice yourself saying, every time a friend asks how you are doing, "I'm overwhelmed with work," or "I hate my job," you can change that sentence to "I am challenged by my job."

  This rewording creates a more empowering truth and dares you to rise to the test. If you find yourself thinking, "I am really paying for my decision to get divorced," you can change the language to something like, "I am investing in a new beginning." Instead of feeling like a victim, you can instead embrace the more positive view that a door to a new life is opening. Words are powerful and how we talk to ourselves has the power to change our lives.

- **The power of "yet."** Just adding the word "yet" to your vocabulary can have a huge positive impact. "I haven't been able to get over my ex" can become "I haven't been able to get over my ex—*yet*." We've changed the outlook from a negative one to one of hope. "I haven't been able to lose weight," can become "I haven't been able to lose weight *yet*." A simple little word with the power to shift our reality.

- **Reframing.** When things don't go well, we have the power to shift our frame of mind around an event or issue. If you find yourself in a panic about an unexpected obstacle that's come up, you might find yourself fretting, saying, "How the heck am I going to make this work? It's impossible!" Take a moment to pause and reframe your reaction.

  Instead of focusing on "how" you're going to overcome it and solve it, first consider "what" you want the best outcome to be: "What will it look like when this is going well?"

  This opens the mind and can create a simple shift with powerful results. Often, when you can find your way out of a negative reaction and into a positive response, you will be surprised how quickly an answer comes.

We all have an "itty-bitty-shitty committee" in our heads that doesn't serve us well. But we also have the power to transform it. When we groom what's inside of us, and free ourselves from the power of the ghosts from our pasts and the stuff that steals our joy, something magical happens. We create a new reality for ourselves, one where we engage in life from a place of optimism and positivity.

Directed Visualization #3

The Flying Cows Dare You to Tame the Stuff in Your Head That Steals Your Joy

The flying cows don't listen to mental blather and rants—they listen to what gives them joy

IMAGINE YOU ARE WALKING *down a country road. It's a beautiful sunny day and the sun feels warm on your skin.*

As you walk, you hear birdsong. A soft warm breeze brushes your cheek. You walk toward the gentle sound of a brook burbling along. You notice a small wooden bridge ahead that looks as if it was built by hand—the intricate design carved on the railings looks like a woven tapestry of leaves and animals.

As you get closer, you notice there is a patch of thyme growing on the righthand side and a lush patch of mint on the other. The fragrance welcomes you and makes you feel embraced and refreshed. You step onto the sturdy bridge, intending to cross it.

But when you get to the middle, you notice there is a round perch on the side with a soft pink velvet pillow that invites you to sit down. Seated comfortably and safely, you now have a front-row view of the sparkling stream below. Golden river birches lean over the stream and a willow languidly dips her leaves into the rippling water. Dragonflies skim the surface of a quiet pool and the rocks bask in the sunshine. You are completely serene in this tranquil paradise.

As you settle deeper into the perch, and take in the scent of thyme and mint, you notice all the little sounds the water makes: a lulling, flowing sound; a soothing cascading as it pours down a series of tumbling rocks; a hushing splattering as water hits a pebble in the middle of the stream; a calming and comforting babble all around.

As you take in all these sounds, your gaze travels to a section of the stream where the water has created a small pond. The water there is calm. So calm, that it reflects the clouds and the blue sky overhead. As you look more closely, you notice something is moving in the reflection. At first, you think it's another dragonfly, or perhaps a flock of birds passing by overhead. Then you look up.

It's the flying cows! They are flying in a perfect circle and kicking their heels to the heavens as if they were dancing in a conga line.

YOU KNOW YOU HAVE ENTERED *a realm your rational mind can't explain, yet you feel at ease and comfortable in this beautiful place.*

The cows continue frolicking as you watch. You are particularly entranced by the strongest of all the cows, Terra, who has a black, sleek coat that glistens in the sunshine. Terra notices you on the bridge and floats down to join you. You are in awe of this amazing, loving beast. Her beautiful jet-black coat shines so much that it has a blueish tint to it. As you lay your hand on her, you can feel the chiseled muscles under her skin and you sense the power and strength she possesses.

Terra lets you know she is here to help you tame the gunk inside your head that dims your light and steals your joy. She shares that this is not a matter of physical strength and that you don't need muscles of steel to pacify the wild broncos inside your head. You can soothe the brutes with a gentle touch, by expressing appreciation for how they have helped you throughout your life, with humor for the absurdity of what they make you do sometimes, and the willingness to let go of what no longer serves you well.

SHE BEGINS BY TEACHING YOU *her favorite breathing technique for calming the mind. She calls it the "Moo Breath." How funny, and appropriate, you think.*

Terra instructs you to take in a deep breath through your nose. While keeping your mouth closed during the exhale, you are to push the air upward, as if it was flowing up your spine, as if it was caressing the inside of your spine on the way up. Continue to push the air through the back of your throat and out your nose. As you do this, make a "MMMOOO" sound with only your breath and without involvement from your vocal cords. It emerges from you like a somber and peaceful snore.

Terra asks you to do it again, but now to expand your inhale and to slow down the exhale. She suggests you repeat it at least ten times. She explains that this technique works because it will not only quiet the mind, but also soothe your entire body, allowing you to relax and reground. She suggests you use it anytime you feel stressed, anxious, or scattered.

You breathe and intone as instructed and feel a stillness permeate your entire body as well as your mind.

Terra then shows you how you can clean out the things cluttering your head—all the heavy stuff that weighs you down.

She asks you to sit sideways on the perch. Your right side faces the incoming water and your left faces the outbound flow that has gone under the bridge. She instructs you to focus on the sound of the water, as if it's coming in through your right ear and then leaving your body through your left ear.

Concentrate on this. Listen. It's as if the gentle burbling of the water is literally flowing through your mind on its way downstream.

Your mind may resist, *like a recalcitrant child having to bathe. It may try to argue with you. You might hear phrases like: "This is silly! Why am I doing this? I have so much to do and I'm wasting my time with this nonsense!"*

Terra reassures you that it's only normal for your mind to resist the first attempt at structure and training. Imagine it is a two-year-old throwing a tantrum.

Focus instead on the burble and babble of the water entering one ear and flowing out the other.

Terra asks you to notice the first negative thought that comes up. Maybe it's anxiety about an upcoming job interview. Or fear of not having enough money. Or jealousy about how someone looked at your significant other. Focus your attention on that negative thought for a few seconds and acknowledge it, recognize that it's real to you.

Then thank the negative thought for what it has taught you, for any lessons learned, and for the times it served you well in the past. Even if you don't know why the thought may have been helpful, by appreciating it you'll find it easier to let it go.

Then smile at the thought. Look for humor in what happened or might happen. For example, how it had you devouring the pint of ice cream in five minutes, or about the ugly shoes you bought when the rants in your head had you doing retail therapy.

The objective here is to remove the heaviness, to lighten up the thought with humor.

And, then just allow the flowing sounds of the water to pick up the thought and to take it away, downstream.

AFTER A WHILE OF LISTENING and focusing, Terra tells you to spin around on your perch. Now you have your left ear facing the incoming water and your right facing the downward stream. Once again, she asks you to observe what mental chatter or rants show up. Whatever it is, don't judge it. Just acknowledge it, thank it, look for the humor in it, and release it.

Terra encourages you to do this cleansing exercise until the thoughts that come up are positive and optimistic.

As she gets ready to rejoin the conga line up in the sky, she lets you know that she is always here for you, that you can come back to the bridge any time you need help releasing negative thoughts and emotions. She also lets you know that it's perfectly okay to seek the assistance of a trusted advisor, or a professional, if you need extra help.

As Terra bids you goodbye, she reminds you that taming the negative talk in your head is best handled gently—with gratitude, laughter, and a genuine willingness to let go of what isn't serving you well.

She lets you know that you have what it takes to tame your thoughts and emotions, and that you deserve a life where you feel uplifted and happy—because you are worthy of joy.

Practice #4:

*H*onor the Light

Within Yourself

My Connection with My Inner Light
Was Lost at the Age of Eight

During the four long years I lived with the nuns, I was treated in ways that no child should have to endure.

These were not soft-hearted nuns; more like boot-camp drill sergeants. They screamed and shouted at us, their faces close to ours. They were always ready to hit us hard if we disobeyed them, or if we just happened to be at the wrong place at the wrong time. They were harsh, intolerant, bitter disciplinarians.

One night there was a lice inspection. All twenty girls in my dorm stood in line with hair parted and heads bent forward, ready to be checked. Yes, the two girls who were inspected before me had lice. By the time the nun turned toward me, she was so furious she didn't even look carefully at my scalp. Instead, she grabbed my long blond hair and swung my head violently around, like a wolf shaking its prey after lunging for the kill. She released me with such force that I went flying and hit the metal footboard of one of the beds.

That night, I cried and cried. No one spoke a word of tenderness or encouragement. All that could be heard in that dorm were my sobs. The next morning, in complete silence, we all had our hair completely chopped off.

During those dark days and months and years, I felt everything I loved had been taken away. I had nothing left from my old life—nothing. Not even what I liked to eat. No eggs from our chickens, a fresh apple just picked off the tree, or a creamy cup of milk straight from one of our cows. Instead, I had to eat whatever disgusting mess the nuns placed in front of me. They didn't care if we didn't like it, we had to eat it or there was hell to pay.

One meal I found especially revolting was a ubiquitous lentil potage. I hated it so much that I would start breaking into a sweat just at the smell of it. One time I was gagging so badly, I could not even force a bite into my mouth. A nun noticed I was not eating and made me stand up by the side of the table so all the girls could watch.

The nun put the plate right under my chin and proceeded to shove spoonful after spoonful into my mouth, even while I was gagging. As she was halfway through, I couldn't keep up with the food and I threw up on my plate. Without flinching, she continued to force-feed me my own vomit.

Those grim years marked me in many ways. They pushed me to question religion, spirituality, the mere idea of God or a higher being. After all, if these nuns were a representation of God on Earth, how could they be so cruel? The more I learned about all the bad things that had been done throughout history in the name of religion, the more I rejected any concept of God. I also blocked any spiritual connection within myself. In my head, spirituality and religion were one and the same, and I didn't want any part of either of them.

When My World Darkened, I Found a Power Source

For many years, I considered myself an atheist. But then, one terrible night, I reconnected with my spirituality again.

I got the call that all parents dread: My son, who had just graduated high school, had been in a horrific car accident. It was night time and he was on his way home when, on a bridge, his car was struck head-on by another vehicle. The other car had entered the bridge while traveling in the wrong direction and the collision happened at such a high speed that both cars were airborne, one landing on the divider and hanging over the side.

Everyone else involved in the accident died on impact. My son was the only survivor.

During that long night at the hospital, not knowing whether my child was going to live or die, I reached for God's hand, humbled and afraid for my child, and for myself, because I didn't know how I could endure life without my son. I begged for a miracle.

And something happened. Suddenly, I felt a calmness come over me. I didn't feel scared anymore. Something told me that I was going to be okay. No matter what happened, I'd be okay.

During that night, my soul connected with something bigger than me: God, Spirit, Universe, Essence, Higher Self, whichever name, it doesn't matter. Because of that connection, I went from utter despair and helplessness to feeling hopeful about what was ahead, empowered by the ability to handle whatever would come our way.

That experience challenged my stance on spirituality. In my mind, I'd painted a picture of a "Higher Power" as an authority figure, like Big Brother watching over me in judgment. But that night my experience was the complete opposite. What I connected to was an accepting, calm, loving energy. I felt protected and empowered—not judged or disciplined.

I kept asking myself, could I have been wrong all this time? Is there a force of some sort we could connect with all the time, and not only in moments of crisis?

I went on a journey of discovery, and I found the answer in silence. It's in the quiet, in the stillness of my mind, when I shut my mouth, turn off my gadgets, ignore my to-do lists, block off all those obligations I think I have, and simply listen to the silence that I can tap into this extraordinary energy, one that fills me with feelings of love, generosity, compassion, kindness, forgiveness, hope, and courage.

I tried many things to help me shed the baggage from my past and the emotional scars from all the things I endured. But the one thing that had the most profound effect on me has been going into this space inside of me where I can tap into this energy.

It has transformed my life.

Thanks to this connection with something bigger than myself, I can find peace when negative emotions, such as anger, grief, and despair, run away with me. I can find patience with myself and others when I am at a point where I want to scream in frustration. Tolerance, when it's a lot easier to judge and criticize. Acceptance, when I find myself resisting what life sends my way. Courage, when I am deeply afraid. Strength when I feel weak and am tempted to give up.

Compassion for others and myself. Hope for a better tomorrow when the world around me seems to spin out of control.

"Now, peace, patience, tolerance, acceptance, courage, compassion, and hope light my way."

Tapping into this powerful force has also shed a light on the way I navigate through life. It has provided me with access to my own internal navigation system—the place inside of me that knows what direction is best for me and what is in my best interest. This has allowed me to make so many good decisions! For example, it helped me decide if I should leave or stay in my job of twenty years, if it would be beneficial to move across the country. It even helped me decide on the house I wanted to buy.

And it told me it was time to open myself up to a romantic relationship again.

Access to this power source inside of me has strengthened my intuition profoundly. Because of it, I've been able to gain insights that I might otherwise be blind to. It has allowed me to experience a higher level of understanding and wisdom.

My life has endured many dark clouds and heavy thunderstorms. I have gone through a lot of heart-wrenching and challenging experiences. But because I developed my ability to connect to my internal light, my higher self, my own true source, I have been able to not only survive but thrive.

I couldn't be more grateful for this gift.

We All Have the Power to Connect to Our Personal Sun

When we feel stuck, one of the ways to help ourselves is by connecting with the personal sun that shines within each of us. Some of us don't get to feel its warmth on a regular basis because the dark clouds of our human experience get in the way and dim its light.

But when we can find a way to part the clouds and look beyond the haze, its rays do shine brightly on us.

It's like flying in a plane on a cloudy, rainy day. Before takeoff, everything looks gray and gloomy. We might even be in the midst of a thunderstorm, surrounded by crashing thunder and terrifying flashes of lightning. But the moment the airplane takes off, and ascends, rises up and up until it breaks through the cloud line, rises up beyond the clouds, it's a whole different day up there. The sun makes everything look bright and cheerful again. Even the dark clouds down below are light-drenched and beautiful.

In the same way, our personal sun is a powerful force. It's the center of our universe, the center of our heart.

There are so many reasons why it's worth spending time strengthening our connection to this force:

- It shines so brightly that it can make everything shimmer with light, even when life appears dull and gloomy.

- It helps to heal us when we are hurt and suffering. It fills us with energy when we are depleted and exhausted.

- It emboldens us to stand tall when we feel crushed. It will show us the way forward.

- It comforts us with its warmth when we feel exposed to the chill from the outside world. It encourages us to grow and blossom despite everything.

- It invites us to come out of our safe cocoon and let go of old layers that hide our inner light. It inspires us to make this world a better place.

- It opens us to our creativity and our intuition. It aligns us with a source of boundless wisdom that will always guide us in the right direction.

We all have access to this unconditional power source of eternal love and infinite wisdom. Regardless of our religion or spiritual beliefs—or lack of—we all have access to it. It's right there, just beyond the clouds of everyday life.

"When we find our quiet, inner place, we open ourselves up to hearing our personal truths and trusting our intuition."

As I said earlier, one of the best ways to connect to it is through Silence. When we clear the debris of daily thinking and feeling, then the light finds its way to us. When we put the outside world on pause and tell "the committee" to be quiet for a few minutes, we feel the gentle clarity of our personal sun.

There are various ways to find Silence. For some people, yoga is their go-to. For others, focused prayer works best. Going for a run or a walk in nature may work well, or the simple practice of daily meditation. But the method we use is not that important. What's important is that we find something that works for us; an activity that brings us to that quiet, inner place. This is a personal matter and each of us must find what works best for us.

The key goal is to quiet our thoughts and calm our emotions. It's only then that we can become open to making a connection with our guiding sun, our inner truth; to trust that it's there to help us. To trust that it is there to guide us.

The secret is to trust our inner sun. When we trust it, instead of fearing or doubting it, our creativity buds. Our intuition blossoms. We find peace, contentment, security, satisfaction, —and a new perspective on life.

When we trust the light of our inner sun, we are no longer caught up in destructive shades of fear, anxiety, guilt, shame, or worry. We are no longer slaves to intrusive, negative thoughts. These thoughts no longer have us on their leash, forcing us to go to places that are not in our best interest.

We are no longer attached to old pain that keeps trying to jab us, and instead we can recognize the teachings from the pain and let go of the rest. We are no longer confused or feel scattered, not knowing which way to turn or where to place our attention. We stop living tangled lives that keep us in a state of confusion and disarray.

When we trust our personal sun, it becomes our guide. Every time we find ourselves at a crossroads in life, it points the way—a friendly, guiding lamp. We get a feeling in our gut that knows the right answer to the questions in our head, questions like, "What direction should I go?" "Who do I need to become?" "Are these people good for me?" This voice deep inside of us knows just what to do at any given time. It's our very own "spidey sense" that intuits which way is best or when something is not quite right.

Trust Your Internal Guidance System

But how do we know the difference between our personal sun and our "committee?"

One of the simplest ways to distinguish the two is by noticing how we feel about each. If we find ourselves in a swirl, worrying about all the things that could go wrong, obsessing about what others will think, feeling shaky about being good enough, taken over by a tornado of negative emotions, and our ego is worried, then we know that our "committee" is ON.

But if we feel inspired by what's ahead, excited about the new opportunity—even if it's a challenge, if we feel calm and composed, if the direction feels right for us, and the greater good, our outlook is positive, we can trust that our inner sun is shining brightly.

The wisdom we get from the force of our personal sun works similarly to the navigation system in our car. When it's turned on, there's no stress about getting to our destination. We don't have to worry. We know we'll get there simply by following the computer voice.

But when we don't have it turned on, and we drive without guidance, we might get lost and end up in the wrong place!

All we need to do is pause, ask it for directions, and listen. Most important, we need to trust it. The guidance we receive might be very different from the norm. It could be telling us the right thing for us is to turn left when everyone is turning right.

We can practice trusting our internal guidance system, our personal sun, by starting with small things, like what to wear in the morning or what to order off a menu. When we trust what feels right, and go with it, we can go on to bigger questions. As we learn to trust it, we gain confidence. We are willing to stand out from the pack instead of blending with it— if that's what the guidance calls for.

Most people don't like standing out, but those who do things that might be considered crazy or unconventional are very often the ones who are most successful and admirable.

They're the ones who allow their inner sun to reveal to them their own light. They're respected and admired because they do what feels natural to them. They don't go against their own nature. And in the process they influence the world in unique and extraordinary ways.

When we are connected to our personal sun, we become grounded in ourselves, we march to our own beat, and we make our own rules for what works and what doesn't work for us. We empower ourselves to take a leap forward. We trust our intuition. We proceed according to our own plan.

This might take us through unchartered territories and down lonely roads, but we never feel lost or alone because we are always guided along the way.

Directed Visualization #4

The Flying Cows Dare You to Reconnect with Your Inner Light

The flying cows trust the force within to elevate themselves above the clouds.

IT IS LATE IN THE EVENING *and you are taking a stroll down a tranquil country lane. You have a lot on your mind. You are trying to decide on a matter that has been gnawing at you. As you ponder the pros and cons of the issue, and feel all the worry and anxiety around the decision that must be made, you encounter the sweet fragrance of roses. You look around to see where the smell is coming from. But in the twilight you can't see any roses.*

As you continue walking, the lovely fragrance continues to escort you along your way. Even though you can't see the flowers, their scent is intoxicating. The path you are on leads you to a little wooden gate. It is exquisitely carved with images of roses and leaves twining around the posts.

You lift the latch on the side of the gate, compelled to see what is on the other side.

As you push through it, you see several winding gravel paths ahead that all go in different directions, with flowerbeds brimming with violets, eglantine, lilies-of-the-valley, and rose bushes lining each path.

You hear water splashing and move toward the sound. Pathways made of old pavers lead to a stone fountain in the center of the garden, where the water flows tranquilly out of the top of the fountain and into the pool of water lilies at the bottom.

As you take in the mix of fresh evening air and the sweet aroma, you find yourself completely relaxed. You sit down on a wooden bench, which has more roses carved into it. Look around this peaceful place. From here you have a view of the whole garden, and you even can see how one path leads directly to a meadow with low grass.

You feel at home here—comfortable and completely at ease.

As YOU LOOK UP, you notice an infinite dark blue sky full of twinkling stars. Your eye catches a pattern of stars that is perfectly aligned, as if it were trying to tell you something.

And then you see them! The flying cows are floating and gliding in the night sky. As they frolic, they draw magical, infinity-shaped figure eights.

You smile at the sight, and you realize you have been transported to a space where anything is possible, where something much bigger than you is at play.

THEN CELESTE, the most dainty and graceful of the flying cows, floats down to join you. You are in awe of her beauty. Her coat is the purest white you have ever seen. It's so shiny and shimmery that it glistens like starlight. Her eyes are a light, celestial blue. Her demeanor is soft and loving and you immediately feel safe and deeply cared for—as if you were in the company of an angel.

Celeste tells you she is there to help you connect with the light within yourself. She is there to help you look for answers to your questions by trusting the wisdom within you. She is going to teach you how to go beyond thinking and feeling and get to a place of true knowing.

CELESTE ASKS YOU *to lean comfortably against the back of the bench. Take a few deep breaths, deep into your belly, and release them. Now picture a pure, white light about two feet above your head. See this light as your own personal sun shining bright on you.*

She asks you to picture this purifying, warm light surrounding you, then surrounding the bench you are sitting on, and then growing to embrace the entire garden. She lets you know that you are in a space where you are sheltered from the outside world, that you are now connected to a bigger network of ultimate wisdom.

Celeste asks you to focus on the matter that is troubling you, perhaps a situation that has you been worrying you and that you are not sure how to best tackle. You can address anything—big or small—with Celeste's loving guidance. Is it time to leave your job? Is this romantic interest the right person for you? What school is a better fit for your child? Should you trust what your coworker or friend is telling you? Should you spend that much money on a pair of shoes? Is it wise to change your diet to be gluten-free?

ONCE YOU PINPOINT THE MATTER *that is nagging at you the most, she asks you to place one hand on your head and to think about all the pros and cons around this decision. She suggests you speak out loud all your thoughts, and she recommends that you don't judge them. There is no right or wrong thought. This part of the process is simply about giving all the stuff inside your head a voice.*

She suggests you begin by saying to yourself, "I think... " And then just roll off all the thoughts that arise in your mind about this matter. For example, if you are trying to decide to stay or leave a relationship your thoughts could look something like this: "I think...my partner is not the person I fell in love with anymore. We have grown apart and we don't share much in common. We make a good team and our children do better with both of us around. I wouldn't be able to afford the mortgage on my own and we would have to sell the house. Our kids would most probably have to change schools. My partner would find someone else, I could end up alone for the rest of my life."

Again, Celeste reminds you not to judge your thoughts, even if they sound crazy, irrational, or random.

ONCE YOU HAVE LET GO *of what you're thinking mind is focusing on, Celeste asks you to now place your hand on top of your heart and this time to focus on all the feelings that you are experiencing as you wrestle with this decision. She suggests* you begin by saying to yourself, *"I feel..."* And then just give all your feelings a voice. Just let each feeling come up and out:

"I feel anxious and nervous about this decision. I am scared to death about making the wrong decision. I feel furious at my partner for not making our relationship a priority. I feel unloved and unappreciated. I worry about my financial security and what the future could look like on my own. My heart hurts just thinking about seeing my partner in a happy relationship with someone else. I dread having to tell our children and worry how they will react. I feel like I failed."

Celeste reminds you to not judge your feelings or yourself for feeling what you feel.

Once you have articulated all the feelings inside of you, Celeste asks you to take a few deep breaths to clear and release all the thoughts and feelings.

THEN SHE ASKS YOU *to put a hand on top of your solar plexus, the spot right on top of your stomach. Focus again on the matter you are trying to decide on. This time you can begin by saying, "I know..." Celeste asks you to just say the first thing that comes to you, to simply trust what comes out of you.*

For example, it could be, "I know it's time for me to leave this relationship," or, "I know this is not the right time for me to leave yet," or, "I know our relationship can recover from this and I want to give it one more try."

Whatever the answer is, Celeste asks you to trust it. To know that it comes from a place of inner wisdom where you are connected to your true self, to your internal guidance system. She reminds you that this is your true voice, that this is coming from a place where your thoughts and feelings have not intervened, and your intuition and connection to a greater force has come through.

As Celeste gets ready to rejoin her friends, she lets you know that the figure eights up in the sky are to remind you that when you connect to what's truly inside of you, you are tapping into a source of infinite wisdom, to a place of positivity and goodness that goes beyond all the thoughts and feelings typical of the human experience.

You are tapping into a powerful force that comes from a source of infinite love.

As she waves goodbye, Celeste lets you know that the gate to the rose garden is always open for you, and that you are welcome to visit her whenever the outside world has you wrestling with tough decisions, when you feel stuck and don't know what is right for you, when the clouds dim your inner light, or when you just need a boost of pure goodness. She is always here to help you regroup and reconnect with that place of purity and holiness within you, with your true essence.

She reminds you that life is better when you go beyond the clouds and connect with your inner light.

Practice #5:

Inspire Your Inner Child to Come Out and Play

I Learned the Hard Way That
I Needed to Lighten Up

As I think back on how I approached my work life, I don't know whether to laugh at myself for being so obsessed or to cringe at the insanity of it all.

Since being a teenager, I had a persistent desire to attain and achieve. Maybe it was my fervent desire to never be poor again. Maybe it was pure ambition. Or, maybe life was preparing me to be financially independent so I could finish raising two kids on my own. Maybe all of the above. Regardless of what drove me, my aspiration to succeed had me constantly seeking the next challenging assignment, the next increase in scope of responsibility, and, of course, the next promotion and the higher paycheck.

Add to this my perfectionism and self-criticism, and the pressure intensified to a point where I typically worked twelve-hour days, and often more. My cell phone and computer were such a part of me that I would go through withdrawal if I didn't have them by me. They would be the last thing I looked at before going to sleep and the first thing I checked upon waking up. Even while on vacation, I was not able to detach and unplug. I was like a trained animal: my ears would perk and twitch to the sound of an incoming email or text.

On top of that, I had to look the part. I took very seriously the motto that I needed to dress for the job I wanted to have. Everything had to be exactly right: hair and makeup had to be stylish and appropriate; outfits polished and classy, yet not boring; accessories had to make a statement without being a distraction....

Talk about pressure!

And then, there also were my personal problems, my home, and the burdens of all the emotional baggage I was dragging.

It made for a dreadful way to go about life.

While I was somewhat aware that this way of life was not sustainable long-term, I was so caught up in it that I didn't know how to break the cycle. Even when my physical body broke down and I became seriously ill, I continued to work. At one point I had nine different doctors working on my case, none of whom could figure out what to do to help me.

My health worsened to a point that I became scared. I lay in a hospital bed, not knowing what the rest of my life was going to look like, or if I was going to have a normal life ever again.

For the first time, I reflected on what might really be happening. I realized I had allowed too many outside obligations to run my life. I was going about my days like an exhausted automaton.

More importantly, I realized I was deeply unhappy.

I had gone through a good portion of my life without acknowledging that life blinks by. Lying there in the hospital one lovely summer afternoon, and not knowing why I was so ill and therefore not having any hope for a cure, I thought about how many summers I might have remaining.

It didn't seem like a lot. And even if there were a few left, would I feel healthy enough to do things I always wanted to do? Would I travel to distant corners of our beautiful planet?

Would I climb the face of a mystical mountain or dive deep into the ocean and explore a coral reef?

Realizing that I might have a severely limited number of summers left was a reality check that hit me like a swift pop in the head. It became the catalyst and motivator to go about my life very differently.

"I began looking at interactions with colleagues as if they were friends on the playground."

I decided to make my well-being a priority. I had nothing to lose! I decided to lighten up and not take myself so seriously. I decided to get out of my own way and take some chances. I decided to enjoy every aspect of my life to the fullest. I promised myself to make it a practice to laugh or smile regularly and to allow my inner child to come out and play at least once a day.

And something very interesting began to happen when I did: All areas of my life transformed.

Emotionally, I started looking at my story with lightness. At times I even laughed about my melodramatic "soap opera," both at work and at home. I stopped worrying so much about making mistakes. I started joking about situations in which I found myself in a pickle, calling them "Maria Moments." I made light of them.

Almost right away, I regained my physical health and became more active, and my daily lifestyle shifted dramatically.

Professionally, I began to look at my interactions with my colleagues as if they were playmates in a school playground. There were still rules to abide by, but this image created space for a sense of humor. I also became more strategic and creative. I found myself looking at work challenges with a different lens that brought to life bolder ideas, solutions, and endeavors.

Culturally, I opened myself to experiences that I would have never considered before, such as hiking Machu Picchu, ziplining in Costa Rica, skydiving, and signing up for ballroom dancing. Without my new perspective on life, I may have missed out on many laughs and many adventures that have opened my mind to different ways of seeing and enjoying what life has to offer.

Personally, I gave my inner child license to point the way for me. Where would it like to play? Eventually, I ended up moving across the country to live near the water in a place where I can enjoy the outdoors every day of the year.

Now I wear what appeals to me and not what I think I need to wear. Socially, I'm more positive and lively. Even people who would typically annoy me don't bother me anymore. I'm able to poke fun at the situations or even call them on their issues with humor.

Romantically, my new approach has opened doors that I kept tightly closed before. I even allowed a special someone into my life, someone who would have never crossed paths with me if I hadn't let go of the heaviness of my past and allowed my playful side to come out, if I hadn't been brave enough to take some chances.

Granting myself permission to be playful and to approach life with a sense of humor has been one of the best things I have done for myself. It not only healed me physically, mentally, and emotionally, but it has completely shifted my outlook on life, from one of unhealthy heaviness to one of healing, lightness, pleasure, and fun.

We Need to Add a Touch of Playful Magic to Everything We Do

Most of us are living very stressful lives.

Our demands at work push us to levels of intensity that at times feel overwhelming. Our clients want what they want, when they want it, without regard for our other competing priorities. Our bosses set objectives that seem unachievable.

Some colleagues may play undercover political warfare, others may annoy us dropping by to tell us their latest melodramatic saga. Then there are those who lack a strong work ethic and expect us to pick up their share. And there's the omnipresent expectation that we should be attached to our phones and computers and be available 24/7.

Our personal lives are not any better. If we have young children, their extracurricular activities keep us hopping from place to place like ping-pong balls. Their arduous homework assignments require hours of attention. And getting them to bed may be nothing short of a wrestling match.

If our children are older, we may obsess over trying to figure out what they are up to, especially since they may no longer confide in us the way they used to. We wonder who they are talking to or dating, who they are driving with, whether they are drinking or experimenting with drugs, or what they are posting and sharing on social media. We are wired to worry.

If that weren't enough, our parents may be getting older and needing our help. Or our partner could be having a mental breakdown.

And of course, the house needs to be cleaned and laundry needs to be done. Someone needs to cook and clean up.

The dog needs to go to the vet. Calls need to be returned. Bills need to get paid.

And then there is Facebook, Twitter, Instagram, and Snapchat to keep up with. There we get to see pictures of people living lives we wish we had and going to exotic places we wish we could afford. Even though deep inside we suspect that they are not as happy as they portray themselves to be—and their lives are not as glamorous as they appear—at that moment our jealousy meters spike and we can't help but feel envious of what they have and resentful of what we don't.

After all of this has put us in a lousy mood, then we come across the newsfeed with the latest political debacle, the terrible calamity that has struck a certain place, the latest terror attack or wave of violence, a crash that killed innocent people, or the latest sexual predator who reminds us that evil exists.

We notice the bags under our eyes from lack of sleep, our discombobulated postures from carrying the world on our shoulders or from sitting too long in front of our computers and the sheer stress of life feels overwhelming.

Sadly, this is the typical routine many of us follow day in and day out. We are like clumsy hamsters on very slippery wheels running at full speed, completely burned out, and feeling stuck and getting nowhere. While we may know it's unhealthy and that it will catch up to us in the form of our work lives taking a tumble, our relationships falling apart, or our health breaking down, we find it hard to shift gears.

Somewhere between childhood and adulthood, we forgot how to play. For most of us, time off means zoning out in front of our screens, binge-watching stressful shows and eating unhealthy food.

What Happened to Playtime?

But imagine if we didn't wait for a physical, emotional, mental, or professional breakdown and instead started introducing humor, levity, and playfulness into all aspects of our lives proactively. What if, without losing sight of our responsibilities and obligations, we created space in our daily lives for fun and lightheartedness? What if we allowed that part of us that is silly—and maybe even a little juvenile—to come out and play?

If we didn't take ourselves so seriously, if we let our hair down and embraced our sense of adventure, how would the "shoulds" and "musts" feel then? If we approached our problems and challenges through the lens of our inner child—and tapped into our imaginations and creativity for fun answers—how would our worries and anxieties play out? If we loved and displayed affection without inhibitions and didn't care if we appeared a little silly and even foolish, how would our relationships flourish?

If we did …

- We might look at our situations as if they were rich material for a stand-up comedy. We might spin our stories and laugh and joke about the absurdity and foolishness of it all.

- We might picture those mean authority figures in our lives who intimidate us as characters in a silly cartoon. Maybe we'd imagine them as sumo wrestlers, wearing only loincloths on a winter day, covered with goosebumps and shivering.

- We might give our imaginations and creativity license to come out and play, to show us new ways of doing things, new directions to be charted, and new horizons to be explored.

- We might replace our brain-numbing screen-time with playtime, and we would have no problem cranking up the music and dancing around our houses like children—and *with* our children.

- We might have fascinating stories to tell about all our adventures and the predicaments we have found ourselves in.

- We might allow our inner child to teach the younger generation in our lives how a belly laugh really feels.

- We might be masters of levity, with the ability to pivot heated debates away from antagonism and into understanding.

- We might walk ourselves off ledges by poking fun at our ability to go from zero to sixty in a matter of seconds.

- We might give bear hugs to the people we love and maybe add a little tickle attack every day.

We Could All Use More Sparkle

The magic of play can make every aspect of our lives better. Humor and laughter heal us. They help us to purge the stuff that hurts deep inside.

Playing can also open up a world of possibilities. Playing with our loved ones, friends, colleagues, and even our pets can strengthen our relationships while creating a space of healthy relaxation, imagination, and creativity.

Playing can also add sparkle to our otherwise mundane lives and can even free us from what keeps us stuck. When we give ourselves license to enjoy the magic of play, everything shifts. Life becomes easier, more entertaining, and enjoyable. Our relationships are more gratifying, our jobs are more fulfilling, our travels are more adventurous, our thoughts are more positive, and our hearts are happier.

Yes, life still blinks by. But now those blinks become a lot more memorable and pleasurable—because they are accompanied by fun and laughter.

Directed Visualization #5

The Flying Cows Dare You to Enjoy the Magic of Play

The playful and adventurous nature of the flying cows allows them to soar through the skies.

IT'S A WARM, SUNNY DAY *and you decide to take a walk to clear your head. As you stroll down a wide country lane, deeply absorbed in thought, you pause to take notice of your surroundings.*

There is nothing, absolutely nothing, but an open road that stretches out into infinity ahead of you!

Fresh, tall grass sways in the breeze on either side of you. There is not even a single tree within sight.

You look up and the sky is an endless sea of blue. There is not a single cloud above. You notice the fresh scent of grass and the light gusts of wind blowing from behind, as if pushing you forward, nudging you to move, to jump, to leap, to explore, to act, to play.

Feeling a little uneasy, you look around, trying to figure out where these persistent gusts are coming from. Is a storm brewing? And that is when you see them, and you start laughing out loud.

The flying cows are playing in the wind.

SOME ARE TWIRLING *and rotating, as if they were gigantic ballerinas, standing on their back legs. Others are running, jumping, and kicking their heels to the heavens. Others are rolling and leaping over each other, creating a playful swirl up in the sky.*

This is the funniest sight you have ever witnessed. You laugh out loud and realize that this is not just any regular day. Today is full of promise and excitement. Something different is going to happen. You have been transported to a place of magic, where anything is possible.

Vespa, the youngest and most playful of the cows, skips down from the blue sky to join you. You chuckle when you see her, and immediately understand why her name is Vespa: she reminds you of a scooter. Her horns grow outward, like the handles on a bike.

She is fast, maneuvers easily, and changes gears quickly

She looks fun, playful, and colorful, and she has a spirit of adventure that thrills you.

She is petite, and her coat is fiery red and sparkly. She has a patch of hair between her horns that grows way longer than the rest of her coat. Some of it stands up, giving her a punk look, and some of it flops down her forehead and swings to one side with an air of mischief.

She has the most glittering reddish-brown eyes you have ever seen. They tell the story of her energy, spunk, and passion for life. She wears a silver nose ring that suits her bold and daring personality. As you look down, you notice that her hooves have a funny bluish tint to them, as if they were painted.

She comes near you and with her nose she messes up your hair, leaving it in total disarray. She tugs at your shirt and messes with your sleeve. She tells you that she is here to help you lighten up, to help you discover the magic of play, to help you reconnect with your adventurous spirit.

VESPA ASKS YOU to stand in the middle of the open country road and to spread your arms out wide, as if you were about to fly. Feel the sensation of the breeze. Feel the puffs of wind blow around you, mussing your hair, making your clothing flap and snap like lively flags.

As you take in the fresh, lighthearted breezes, Vespa begins to skip in circles around you. She nudges you to spin around as if you were dancing with her. She reminds you to let go of all inhibitions and hang-ups. There is no one observing you on this isolated country road. There is no one to pass judgment on anything you do or say. There is no right or wrong. All you need to do is to dance with the wind, to allow your inner child to come out and play, to let yourself go, to laugh out loud, sing, shout, squeal with joy.

To just let yourself be.

NOW YOU ARE OUT OF BREATH and a little dizzy from all the turning and whirling. You slow down as Vespa asks you to look at the open road ahead and to imagine it as a horizon full of possibilities. There are so many places you could go, *people you could meet, things you could do, adventures you could experience, games you could play, new creations you could bring to life, even new ways you can live your life.*

Then Vespa asks you to envision what you would be doing if responsibilities didn't get in the way, if technology didn't distract you, if the opinions of others didn't matter, if money was not an issue. What would your inner child be doing right now, if it had completely free license to play?

Vespa then asks you to think about that area of your life where you are playing it too safe, where you are too structured and constricted and not taking risks. What would this aspect of your life look and feel like if you leapt out of the security of what you know?

Then she asks you to think about a project or a challenge you have not been able to solve and to look at it through the eyes of your inner child, to look at it as a game. Perhaps imagine yourself sitting on the floor with all your ideas spread around you and let your imagination run wild. What new possibilities could come to life if you looked at your problems through a playful lens?

Little Vespa then asks you to think about a situation in your life that has been gnawing at you. Is there a person in your life who pushes all the wrong buttons? She asks you to look at the relationship more playfully.

What if you were a stand-up comedian doing a skit on your situation? How can you use humor and playfulness to lighten up the interactions with this person? Could you spin the story so you can laugh at yourself or at the situation?

Then Vespa asks you to look at yourself, how you dress, how you do your hair, maybe the style of glasses you wear, or how you carry yourself. She asks you to dismiss all your preconceived ideas of what you need to look like or think you should look like.

What would make you smile every time you see yourself in the mirror? What would feel good to you?

As Vespa continues to run around you, playfully kicking up her heels and at times standing on her back legs as if she were popping a wheelie, she reminds you that life blinks by and that it's a lot more fun when you don't take yourself too seriously, when you take time to enjoy the things that make you smile.

Before she gets ready to fly back to her friends, she asks you to turn around and to focus on the long road that you have walked.

REFLECT ON YOUR JOURNEY *through life, your past. Look at all the left and right turns that brought you to this place, all the choices you made along the way to help you arrive where you are in this moment. Now fill your heart with gratitude for all the events that happened and the people who showed up in your life—everything that has helped to make you who you are today.*

And then she asks you to turn around one more time and to face the open road ahead. This is your future. Imagine all the possibilities ahead of you. Smile.

As she waves goodbye, Vespa tells you that you can always find her playing with the wind on this wide, open road. You are welcome to visit her every time life feels burdensome, heavy, and complicated, or when the world around you has lost its sparkle.

She mimics a ballerina spin in midair and laughs at you. In that laugh, you hear her wisdom: life is a lot more fun when you grant yourself permission to enjoy the magic of play.

Practice #6:

Grow High-Caliber Relationships—They Matter!

I Underestimated the Power
Others Could Have Over Me

I was reunited with my parents in the United States at age 12, just as I was going into seventh grade. I joined them in a small Spanish community in New Jersey.

Throughout my tumultuous adolescence, my parents had a saying that really annoyed me: "Show me who you spend time with, and I'll show you what you'll turn into."

They used it frequently to limit the pool of people I could be friends with. While I resented it at the time, looking back, I can't blame them for trying to protect me in any way they could. We lived in a city notorious for drugs and violent crime. As immigrants who didn't speak English, my parents must have lived in constant fear of what could happen to me if I wandered outside of our familiar community.

It was only later in life that I came to understand the deeper wisdom behind their words, and I learned the hard way the power that others can have over me.

For a long time, I was surrounded by people who were not always a good influence on me. They didn't have sound moral compasses or have my best interests at heart. They were judgmental, complainers, and gossipers.

But when I was with them, I found myself behaving the same way they did. I would get caught up in their melodramas and complaints and criticisms.

I didn't realize how damaging these relationships were to me until I began to be sabotaged by them. When I started doing better professionally, I became the focus of their mean gossip. They would make me feel bad about my achievements and insecure about my abilities.

For example, when I was promoted to executive level, malicious gossip was spread that since I wasn't smart enough to get to that level I must have been sleeping with someone at work.

I was mortified when I heard the rumor, and deeply hurt. But even while it was obvious to me that the people spreading this lie were noxious, I couldn't turn my back on them. Some were family members, others were close family friends, and I cared about them, despite their behavior. I even loved some of them.

It wasn't until my husband died that I was able to see clearly how damaging the relationships were to me. Because of the way he died, many people turned on me with a viciousness that tore at me beyond belief. They blamed me for his suicide.

One of the most vicious stories was that my husband had killed himself because he found me in bed with another man. This lie and the betrayal from people I thought I loved became almost too much for me to bear.

The fabrications spread like wildfire across the community and even tainted the minds of hundreds of people I barely knew. Many came to the wake simply to make it known how much they loathed me. They did not whisper their contempt, *they hissed out loud*, making sure even my children heard. They wrote nasty comments on sympathy cards.

I was enduring the most painful moment of my life, and on top of that I was hated by people I had thought were my friends.

The experience was shocking and devastating.

Luckily, there were a select few who stood by my side when everyone else shunned me. They held me up when I felt too weak to stand tall on my own. They believed in me unconditionally when no one else would. They brought sunshine my way when I was in my darkest moments. Thanks to these few high-caliber friends and relatives, I was able to rebuild my life.

"You are judged by the company you keep. Their words and their actions will affect you. So, be choosy."

But sometime later, in a moment of epiphany, I realized that I was still allowing other people to dictate who I would or would not spend time with. The toxic people had exited my life because they chose to, and the few good ones who remained also made that choice on their own.

It was not because I had deliberately decided who was in and who was out. Thankfully, I ended up with a few good ones who helped me get back on my feet, but it was not because I proactively and thoughtfully made that choice.

That realization was a life-changing moment. Right then and there I promised myself that I was taking my power back. I was going to take control of my personal space going forward. I was going to be very choosy about who deserved to be in my life, who would have the opportunity to influence how I feel, what I think, and even what I do.

But most importantly, I decided I was going to develop a strong relationship with myself; one where I treated my personal space as sacred. I decided to allow into my inner circle only those high-caliber individuals who treated me with dignity and respect and would bring positivity into my life.

It was then that I realized that my parents' old saying, "Show me who you spend time with, and I'll show you what you'll turn into," had profound wisdom in it.

Since that time, I am very careful about who I allow into my life. I have learned to quickly assign people into three categories based on how they affect me: negative, neutral, or positive. The negative relates to those who leave me feeling depleted and drained. These are my poison and I look for ways to protect and shield myself from them. The neutrals are those who don't affect me in either a positive or negative way. The positive ones are those who leave me feeling energized and feeling good about life. These are my fuel, these are the people I gladly open my doors to.

Today, I am drama-free and my life is filled with many wonderful relationships that are empowering, trusting, powerful, healing, and fun. Looking back, these high-caliber relationships developed naturally once I decided to honor my personal space and began treating it as sacred.

We All Need "Door Openers," "Guiding Lights," and "Safety Nets"

When we feel stuck, at the root of the issue we will most likely find a relationship problem. Regardless of whether they are social, family, work, professional, or with our soulmates, positive relationships are crucial to our long-term level of happiness.

The people in our lives have the power to influence us in seen and unseen ways. To some degree, their world becomes a part of ours.

If the people we spend the most time with are negative and toxic, they contaminate us. Our lives are full of drama, with something destructive always happening around us. Our needs and what is important to us always come last. These people are with us for as long as we have something that matters to them. Once we don't, they will abandon us, ignoring any despair they leave in their wake.

But if the people we spend the most time with are positive, their optimism and cheerful outlook on life is contagious. There is a lot of laughter in our lives. We feel energized and our internal wells are filled to the brim with courage, confidence, and optimism about the future. We feel challenged and inspired. We feel respected and honored. We can then become the best version of ourselves—a happy and fulfilled version.

Imagine how great life would be if you worked for people who believed in your skills and talents, and stretched you, without breaking you, to your full potential? If your colleagues became your cheerleaders and supported you in your dreams and aspirations? If your significant other treasured your heart and created a safe space for you to be your authentic self without fear of being judged? If your dear friends surrounded you and sheltered you from life's storms, even if those storms were your own doing? If your mentors bolstered your confidence and reminded you of your special gifts and why it's important to put them to good use? If your spiritual guides nourished your mind and soul?

We all have the power to create a life for ourselves in which we weed out the negative relationships and nurture new high-caliber ones. We just need to empower ourselves to stand strong in our conviction to honor our personal space, to treat it as if it is holy and worthy of reverence, a place no one can enter without the utmost respect and appreciation.

Positive relationships come in many forms but there are three categories that spread across all our other relationships: the "Door Openers," "Guiding Lights," and the "Safety Nets." When we proactively nurture these categories across our professional, personal, social, and spiritual relationships, the quality of our lives is elevated significantly.

"Door Openers" are the people who literally open doors for us. They pick up the phone to make a call to get us interviews, hard-to-get appointments, or sales calls; they get us invited to key life-changing events; or they may set us up on blind dates with other singles. They might tell us about job openings that would be perfect for us.

They're the ones who take chances on us and are willing to put themselves out there. They keep their eyes open for things or opportunities that would be of benefit to us, often without us even asking them to.

"Guiding Lights" are the people who point the way during times of uncertainty or darkness. They are there when we don't know which way to go, or we don't have the answers we need to make wise decisions, or when no matter what we do we just can't make things work. It might be jobs we haven't been able to get, elusive promotions, coworkers who drive us crazy, people we care about but can't connect with, family members who get under our skin, or pesky health issues.

"Guiding Lights" are there for us when we feel overwhelmed and we need perspective. They show up to help us to navigate the rocky terrain before us or when we need sage advice.

They are there when we make mistakes and we need guidance on how to make things right. They offer other reference points for us to consider as we weigh our options when deciding about which direction to go in. They help us see alternatives, fresh viewpoints, or even our own blind spots.

"Safety Nets" are the people who catch us when we fall. Life is a rollercoaster ride, with plenty of twists and turns and unexpected loop-the-loops. We all go through times in our lives when we trip and fall, crash and burn. These are the people who stick around when the going gets tough, who provide a shoulder to cry on, act as sounding boards when nobody else will listen, offer us a leg up—such as a temporary job if we lose ours—and support us till we get back on our feet.

"Safety Nets" are special, sacred people. They're hard to come by, but once they come into our lives, we never forget them. We all go through dark moments. And when we do, we need people to extend willing and loving hands to get us back on our feet.

Nurturing Our High-Caliber Relationships

"Door Openers," "Guiding Lights," and "Safety Nets" are classes of high-caliber relationships that are important to our lives. It's smart to nurture these relationships in every way possible.

For example, we all need "Guiding Lights" who are experts in our fields of work and who can give us perspective around our work lives, but don't stop with them. We can proactively nurture other "Guiding Lights" who can give us fresh perspectives in dealing with problems related to our children or aging parents, or with our partners.

The goal is to be proactive about developing and growing these relationships so that they are there for us when we need them. If we build them long before they're necessary, and nurture and honor them all the way along, they'll always be there when we need them.

But … we need to be careful that we don't gravitate to people who look, act, and think the same ways that we do, as that can be very limiting.

Ideally, our relationships include diverse ranges of gender, age, race, profession, industry, religion, and so on. This way we ensure that we are presented with possibilities we don't know of or haven't yet considered. This helps us become more diverse in our thinking and more flexible in our choices.

High-caliber relationships are two-way streets and they require effort. We need to grow them by caring for and feeding them on a regular basis. But having them in our lives will elevate and uplift us to higher ground. When we are surrounded by positive and healthy relationships, there will be a lot of laughter in our lives. We will feel energized and our internal wells will be full to the brim with courage, confidence, and optimism about the future. We will feel challenged and inspired. We will feel respected and honored. We will become the best versions of ourselves—happy and fulfilled versions.

Directed Visualization #6

The Flying Cows Dare You to Honor Your Personal Space

The flying cows are selective
About who they fly with—and soar
higher because of it.

IT'S A CLOUDLESS SUMMER DAY *and you feel the warmth of the sun as you walk through a meadow filled with marigolds. It seems like a sea of yellow that glows and glimmers as the sun beams on the flower petals.*

The mix of the welcoming smell of the warm dry earth with the pungent scent of marigolds is a little intoxicating and yet invigorating at the same time. It's so quiet here. There are no birds chirping and not a single bee buzzing. It's total calmness.

As you make your way through the marigolds, you come across a beautiful old stone well. A silver manual crank right above it can be used to raise a wooden bucket with tin brackets around it.

A two-way wooden roof sits on top, as if shielding the water from debris from the outside. This roof is not just any roof, it's a work of art, with many small pieces of wood coming together to create an intricate, harmonious design. Someone took a lot of care in putting it together. Every stone is placed just right to bring to life this circular masterpiece.

To the side of the well sits a wooden bench that invites you to rest and enjoy the view of the quilt of marigolds in the meadow down below.

As you sit there, you notice a shadow, as if a cloud is passing overhead, but as you look up, you realize that, behold, it's the flying cows! They move playfully as they form the shape of a perfect heart.

YOU CAN'T HELP BUT SMILE. *You know you have entered a realm you don't understand, but it doesn't matter.*

You feel at ease here—as if in this warm, marigold oasis you are in the company of good friends.

Avé, the most colorful of the flying cows, comes down to join you by the well. She lets you know she is there to help you see how the relationships in your life are affecting you, and to empower you to honor and love yourself enough to be discerning about who you invite into your inner circle.

As you stroke her warm coat, you can't help but admire this magnificent beast. Avé's coat has many different shades, as if she were a collection of colors and attributes from all the other six cows, but they come together in a way that is uniquely her own. You can feel her physical strength perfectly balanced by an inner warmth that tells you her heart is full of love and kindness.

You also sense a profound inner wisdom that comes from an old soul that knows a thing or two about life. Yet, at the same time, there is a sparkle in her eyes that is typical of a playful child. As you admire her extraordinary uniqueness, Avé confirms that she represents a blend of the other six flying cows, that she is an amalgamation of all of her closest friends. She also lets you know that you, too, are a reflection of the people you spend the most time with. That these people affect you in ways that are obvious to the eye but also in ways that are unseen, like your mood, disposition, and even the way you think and behave, and the choices you make.

Avé lets you know that the quality of your life relies heavily on the caliber of the people around you and that it's in your best interest to be very selective, to bring into your inner circle only the people who uplift you, bring out the best in you.

Then Avé asks you to think of yourself as if you were the beautiful well here by your side, and to make a mental note of all your relationships: personal, professional, romantic, social, and spiritual. Now, focus on the ones you invest the most time with. Thinking of each one, figure out who fills your well with experiences and feelings that uplift and enrich you and leave you feeling refreshed, full, and feeling good about yourself and your life. Now consider the people who drain your well dry, who deplete you and leave you feeling empty, exhausted, stressed, and down on life.

BEFORE YOU DO ANYTHING *ELSE with the list, Avé asks you to focus on the well again. Notice how much care went into creating and decorating the walls that protect it and into the beautiful roof that shields it. See that there is a limited amount of* fresh, cool water inside it. If more water is taken out than is replenished, the well will go dry. She reminds you that you are like the well: you also need to build walls and shields that protect you from being depleted.

Then Avé asks you to focus on the list of those who drain you and don't put much back into your well. Who is on that list: People from work? Perhaps a complicated friend? Your significant other? Your father or mother? Your child?

She asks you to go through each of the names on your list, one by one, and to ask yourself if these people have potential to change. If you had a conversation with them and let them know how they are impacting you, would they be willing to modify their behavior? Would they care enough about you to change their ways?

For those who can, Avé encourages you to find the courage to have that conversation. You owe it to yourself.

For those who are lost causes and there is no hope for change, Avé asks if you can move them out of your life. If you can, she recommends you come up with a plan for each person depending on the role they play in your life.

For example, if your boss is professionally immature and sucks the life out of you all day long, can you find a different job? If your friends are always stuck in negativity, can you distance yourself by just moving them to the "social buddies" *category? If a relative is totally toxic, what can you do to break the connection?*

Then there are those people who drain your well, yet you feel you can't remove them from your life because they are family, or for other personal reasons. Avé recommends that you be pragmatic and realistic, to accept that they will always take and not give. They will not change.

Instead of hoping for a change in behavior that will not come, focus instead on proactively finding ways to limit their drain on you. For example, if there is a very close family member you love dearly but who hasn't been able to let go of a trauma from the past, find ways to be exposed to that person only in small doses.

More important, put in place a way to receive an immediate recharge for yourself after being with them.

Avé shares with you that the yellow marigolds are natural pest repellants, and suggests you channel the marigold and find creative ways to repel the pests in your life that minimize your growth. She also reminds you that while it might feel a little weird at first to make changes that protect your boundaries—especially if you are naturally wired to be a giver—it will be worth it in the long run.

She then asks you to pivot your attention to the people who fill your well. Picture yourself spending most of your time with those who bring out the best in you, and who inspire you to be the best version of yourself. These people challenge your thinking and open your mind to new possibilities. They motivate you to do things you don't feel comfortable doing yet, and encourage you to live life to the fullest. They stimulate your creativity and vision for how to make this world a better place and are ready to be there for you whenever you need them.

IMAGINE YOURSELF *with high-caliber people, Avé says, people who see you as their equal and in relationships that are honored and valued. She asks you to imagine how wonderful that would feel.*

As she gets ready to rejoin her flying friends, she reminds you to come back to the well to visit her every time you find yourself feeling drained by the people in your life and you need calmness and peace to regroup and reground.

As she returns to the cows hovering in the formation of the beautiful heart in the sky, she lets you know that the heart shape is to remind you that the highest caliber relationship of all is the one you have with yourself. When you love, respect, and honor yourself, then you are naturally selective about who you allow in to your life—and who you deem high-caliber enough to influence and shape who you are and who you will become.

Practice #7:

*H*elp Others Soar Higher

I Didn't Believe I Had What it Took
to Make a Difference in the World

For most of my life, I subscribed to the attitude that there was only so much I could do to improve the lives of others. I volunteered at local charities and donated what I could through work. And while it felt good, I didn't know how to go beyond that. My contributions felt small. But what more could one very busy person do?

Then one day I was shown how even just one person can make a truly life-changing difference to others, to the world, and to themselves.

A friend persuaded me to go to an event during which the speaker droned on about how one single person can improve the lives of millions. As I listened, the chatter in my head kept arguing with him. I kept thinking of all the reasons why I alone couldn't do much to help other people. Maybe I could help one person here and there, but I didn't have it in me to touch the lives of many.

The chatter—that annoying "committee" again—continued: "I don't have time for this nonsense." "I am an extremely busy person with a ton of responsibilities." "This does not apply to me or my life."

Then suddenly all the lights in the auditorium went out. The room became pitch black—we couldn't see anything aside from the red exit signs. I began to feel nervous and anxious about being in total darkness. What was going on? In a very calm voice, the speaker instructed us to retrieve a small candle that had been taped to the bottom of our seats.

On the stage, he struck a match and lit a small candle he held in his own hand. He said to pay close attention to how one single candle could light up the whole room. Then he walked over to two people in the front row, lit their candles, and asked them to pay it forward.

In less than three minutes, more than 200 candles had been lit and infused the entire auditorium with a bright glow.

My negative chatter was silenced at once. I saw that if one single candle could light up hundreds within minutes, then, with enough time, one person could indeed influence positive change and transform the lives of millions.

That First Candle Shed More Light Than I Ever Expected

The experience was transformative for me. The small exercise inspired me to use the pain I endured, the tears I cried, the triumphs I enjoyed, and the lessons I learned to help others who could benefit from my experiences and perspective.

That night I began writing this book.

That night also helped me to realize that making a difference is not only about the grand gestures. It's about all the little things that make a big difference: a kind word to the cashier at the grocery store; the confidence-boost to the coworker; the unexpected tip to the trash collector; or a random note to a loved one, letting them know how special they are.

As I began to put into practice the idea of uplifting everyone I encounter, and making sure that they were in a better place after they interacted with me, I started noticing that by spreading positive energy without an agenda or consideration as to whether they deserved it, I myself was also benefiting.

My mood improved after each interaction. I would feel better about my own circumstances and grateful for what I had.

Often, I would walk away with a new nugget of wisdom or fresh perspective that enlightened my thinking and my creativity.

I was finding these boosts of positive energy so beneficial that they became like "mood medicine" for me. Every time I found myself in a funk, I gravitated toward doing something for someone else. The dosage would depend on the degree of my funk. If things were particularly bad, I would roll up my sleeves and sign up for a larger cause I was passionate about. Without fail, I would walk away feeling much better.

Some of these "mood medicine projects," as I started calling them, not only reset my outlook, they reset my reality.

One of the boldest and most transformational changes came on the heels of my decision to leave corporate America.

I was feeling uneasy about what was next for me. I had been with the company for most of my adult life, and while I knew moving on was the right thing for me, the idea of starting something new, and not knowing if it was going to work out or not, had me feeling rattled and anxious.

A friend of mine travels each year to Manila, Philippines, to engage in volunteer work. I decided to meet him there. The plan was to raise funds before we left and, once there, to look for ways to help the homeless, local orphanages, and the sick children at a local hospital. Given that I know a thing or two about being poor, and having spent several years of my early life in a convent, I felt well equipped to handle what I was signing up for.

What was waiting for me was a reality check that not only gave me fresh perspective on what I did for a living, but reset my whole perspective on life.

By Giving, I Received More Than I Could Imagine

My introduction to Manila was an assault on all my senses. As we left the airport and headed toward the impoverished parts of the city, I encountered traffic unlike any I had ever seen before. Not even gridlock traffic in New York City came close to this. The road was a cacophony of cars, trucks, mopeds, tricycle taxis, and jeepneys, all competing for the next inch forward.

While this dizzying confusion was taking place, pedestrians zigzagged in and out traffic, gambling their lives just to cross the road. The humidity soaked into my clothes and hair and my skin began to feel as though a damp film had formed over it. The pollution could not only be smelled, I could taste it in my mouth. But the worst part was witnessing the children, clearly undernourished, in ripped clothes and bare feet.

While my first impressions of Manila were heartbreaking, the days that followed were even harder. As I took the first tour of the children's ward at the local hospital, I encountered the worst of the human condition. Sometimes it took every little bit of self-control not to burst out crying. There were children with cancer who were dying because the hospital staff couldn't give them the treatment they needed. Those who stood a chance of surviving would probably die anyway, because they lived in towns far from Manila and would not be able to return for ongoing treatments. If they did, they would have to travel on public transportation for many hours, exposed to germs that their weakened immune system wouldn't be able to fight off.

The hospital was so crowded that one small room might be shared by ten children and their families. Three sick children could be found lying across a single twin-size bed. Bathrooms were available, but only all the way down a long, crowded hallway. As a parent, it was particularly distressing to witness the anguish that these parents were enduring.

My time in Manila became a turning point for me. Nothing mattered more to me than trying to ease the intolerable burden of poverty, illness, death, and grief that affects most people who live on this planet.

For the rest of my stay, I helped to feed homeless people. I contributed what I could toward improvements that would keep sick children more comfortable. I helped to fund and organize programs that ran halfway houses where traveling families could stay while their child received medical treatment. I knew my deeds would not change the whole world, but I hoped they would make a small difference in easing the suffering of those I met.

They made a huge difference for me.

I returned to the U.S. from Manila freed from layers of superficiality that in retrospect made me feel empty and worthless. After seeing firsthand how a large percentage of our planet lives, I realized that I could do without most of the things I had always thought were essential to my happiness.

It became clear that I had been working too hard to afford things that didn't bring joy into my life. For the first time, I felt free from the control money had had over my life all my adult life. I was inspired to look for a better way to make a living that wasn't driven primarily by how much it paid.

That trip also helped me to deal with personal crises in a different way. My painful childhood experiences didn't seem so awful after witnessing so much misery. New challenges seemed manageable.

For example, within two weeks of getting home, both my parents had medical emergencies. In the past, I would have felt overwhelmed by the responsibility and drama. Now I was grounded and calm, grateful for having the resources and the excellent medical teams available to care for them.

Making a difference in the lives of others has become an important part of my daily life, not only because it's the right thing to do but also because I get so much in return. Sharing my time, talents, experience, and money to spread empathy, compassion, and care has become one of my most rewarding accomplishments.

It keeps me grounded in the things that really matter. When other aspects of my life have my head swirling, it opens my heart to the human experience, which in turn helps me connect with others in a deeper way. It keeps me humble and appreciative of all the blessings in my life. And it gives my life meaning and connection to a higher purpose.

Each of Us Has the Power to Create a Movement

The best antidote for feeling stuck is to roll up our sleeves and channel the emotions inside of us toward something that helps others. If we pause to think about those turning points that catapulted positive change throughout history, there was always a person behind each one.

It was that one person who stood for what they believed, who took the time to act, who seized the opportunity to make a change, and, as a result, improved the quality of life for, or saved the lives of, many people.

Each of us has a movement inside of us that is waiting to be ignited.

The parents who have lost a child to a drunk driver may channel their grief toward preventing the same thing from happening to others. The person who was bullied as a child may channel their rage by establishing an antibullying program. Those who endure an illness or lose a loved one may channel their pain to raise funds toward treatment and prevention of that particular illness. Those who have experienced legal injustice may leverage their rage to rally for others who are in the same position.

We all have experienced situations that we can tap into as sources of inspiration and as catalysts for change. There's usually at least one thing that makes our blood boil every time we think about it; a memory that keeps coming back to haunt us, events in which we felt powerless, or images in our heads that can't be erased.

We all have something that can motivate us, propel us. Traditionally "negative" emotions—like anger, fear, shame, and helplessness—can, alongside love and a sense of humanity, become solid platforms for inspiring positive transformation.

Imagine what would happen if we all became part of an existing movement or began a movement of our own. What if each one of us signed up to find a cure for a particular illness or to raise positive awareness about an issue that might be typically taboo? Imagine presenting solutions for injustice, oppression, and discrimination, making a dent in poverty, driving social improvement and political change, or uniting for peace.

Our individual and collective efforts make this world a better place.

As we do this, we come to know what we stand for and who we stand with. Our values become evident, our ethics and moral compasses are front and center, and our determination becomes our flagship.

We just need to be willing to dedicate our time, talents, resources, and our voices to that one cause.

While these types of movements create waves that ripple positive change across the world, we can also engage in movements that touch one person at a time. These improve the situation of an individual and can trigger in them a chain reaction that propels them to pay it forward, creating a cascading effect along the way.

In short, we have the power to create a movement with each interaction. We simply need to pause and observe what is truly happening with each person we encounter. When we do, we might notice the anxiety of a friend who seems weepy, or the loneliness in the eyes of an older family member, or the confusion of an overwhelmed coworker.

Imagine how relieved would the weepy friend be if she could trust someone with her problems? How happy would the lonely family member be if he got a visit or an invitation to go out for lunch? And think how relieved the overwhelmed coworker would be if she were offered some help with her responsibilities.

Now imagine the positive impact that all these individuals could create when they pay it forward to all the other people they touch.

When we do good without seeking gain or a return on investment, our actions become forces for good that can benefit loved ones and strangers alike.

Our situations, no matter how bad they are, will no longer seem so dire when we witness the realities of life for others who have much greater difficulties. When we connect personally with those less fortunate, it helps us gain perspective on the things that really matter.

Regardless of the size of our gestures, every time we actively participate in creating moments that touch the lives of others in a positive way, we also enrich our own.

We all have the power to help others soar higher, we all have it within ourselves to be forces for good, we each have what it takes to become that candle that lights up rooms, homes, neighborhoods, cities, countries—and even the planet.

Let's start a movement for goodness!

Fly High!

Directed Visualization #7

The Flying Cows Dare You to Help Others Soar Higher

The flying cows show others how they, too, can soar to new heights.

IT'S A BEAUTIFUL DAY *outside—but you are not yourself. Things are not going your way and the world feels heavy and burdensome.*

You decide to take a walk to clear your head and gain perspective.

As you wander farther into the country, sprays of wildflowers greet you along the way. Their aromatic scent invites you to breathe deeply. Take in the fragrance and beauty of all the lovely bouquets that Earth has so creatively arranged all around you.

As you begin to hear the burbles and splashes from a stream nearby, you notice a patch of springy grass that looks like the perfect spot to lie down.

Rest your head on the bouncy grass, feel the warmth from the sunshine on your skin, listen to the soothing sounds of the flowing water, and inhale the calming aroma of the wildflowers.

You notice a tiny hummingbird fluttering nearby. It is so very small, and yet also so mighty. Then your eyes travel to some honeybees busily buzzing from flower to flower. How hard they work for just one teaspoon of sweet honey!

From the corner of your eye, you notice a big shadow traveling over the grass. Startled, you sit up and watch in amazement as the flying cows dance gracefully down through the air to land on the springy grass by the edge of the stream.

YOU ARE IN TOTAL AWE *of these magnificent creatures. They are all so different in color, shape, size, age, and attitude, yet they all seem to complement each other perfectly.*

As you watch them graze and drink from the stream, Gracey, the most mature and kind of the flying cows, sees you and lopes over to stand calmly at your side.

Her salt-and-pepper coat is longer and softer than the other cows'. It hangs on her as if it were a shaggy angora sweater.

As you reach out and gently touch it, your fingers feel like they are caressing pure cashmere.

She reminds you of a sweet and loving grandma. Her deep, silver-gray eyes tell stories of old hardships, pain and losses, of endurance, compassion, humility, and being of service to others.

Gracey is a powerhouse of wisdom and grace.

She tells you that she is there to help you reconnect with that part of you that has the power to channel your energy toward doing good; on making a difference.

Gracey lets you know that she is there to help you see that inner peace and bliss come from standing up for worthy causes and being of service to others without expecting anything in return.

Then Gracey asks you to think about that instance in your life that hurt the most; that time that left scars that run deep, either physically, mentally, emotionally, or even spiritually. When you endured something that made you feel unsafe. When you witnessed something that still haunts you. When your life changed forever.

Gracey then asks you to label the emotions you feel when you recall that time.

There is no right or wrong—it's okay to let yourself feel as raw as you need to in order to relive that moment. What are the feelings that first pop into your mind? Are they anger, fury, fear, terror, heartache, anguish, powerlessness, shame, guilt?

As you begin *to feel uncomfortable, Gracey lets you know that you are safe here with her. She asks you to take a deep breath, to hold it, and then to exhale slowly. Breathe in again, deeply, exhale again slowly, and repeat this cycle several times until you feel more relaxed.*

She lets you know that this is the moment when you can become a force for good. You can empower yourself and channel what you are feeling toward a worthy cause, toward something that can help others. This is the moment when you can access that force within and use it to inspire yourself to stand for something or to stand with someone. What is that worthy cause you are passionate about?

Gracey lets you know that you have what it takes to make change happen and asks you to think about how you can help. How can you use your time, money, experience, talents, passion, and voice to drive the transformation that is needed?

Then Gracey asks you to place a hand on your heart and to reconnect with it, to acknowledge what is happening to it. If yours feels broken, she reminds you that a broken heart is an open heart. Let all that old pain empty out, let go of the poison inside of you so your heart can heal from the inside out and be whole again. She then suggests you forgive and let go.

If you are not able to forgive yet, Gracey suggests you repeat the following mantra: I am a stronger and a better person because of this.

She murmurs, "If you can't let go, then at least let it be."

Gracey asks you to take a deep breath, to inhale the sweetness of all the aromas around you, and to exhale all the old stuff that doesn't belong in your heart anymore. She asks you to repeat this until you feel relaxed and at ease.

Then Gracey lets you know that you have the power to improve the lives of all who you touch. She shares her favorite practice with you and encourages you to make it a part of all your interactions: Make sure you leave every person with whom you come in contact in a better place. Simply by giving a much-needed compliment, a dose of optimism, a boost of confidence, or just letting someone know he matters and he is loved. Silently send positive energy to all those you cross paths with.

As Gracey gets ready to go back to her sister cows by the edge of the stream, she reminds you that, just like the honeybees buzzing around the wildflowers, it's important to share the sweetness of life. You have the power to spread compassion, kindness, hope, and positivity with the rest of the world. When you do, life shines a tender light on you, and it heals you.

She reminds you that you are welcome to come by the stream to visit her any time your heart feels heavy and things are not going the way you wished they would.

As Gracey rejoins the rest of the flying cows, she lifts off from the ground as a majestic beast and begins to soar through the skies. Then, one by one, the rest of the cows follow her as if they were a flock of magnificent birds in exquisite formation.

As she waves goodbye, she shares one last nugget of wisdom: "Soar high, live your life in a place of grace and kindness with yourself, with others, and with the world."

4

YOU Can Fly High

My heart is full. I feel grateful. I am happy.

These are the thoughts that pop into my head as I sit in my new backyard, gazing at the stillness and sparkle of the deep blue lake spread out in front of me.

The peaceful sky overhead is dotted with a few white clouds that look like piles of bouncy cotton.

The birds are putting on quite a show for me. Duck families swim around with their young, several cranes groom themselves by the water, finches and sparrows chirp a well-orchestrated symphony up in the trees, and a couple of friendly hummingbirds keep me company as they enjoy the sweetness of the pink hollyhocks nearby.

As I sit in the shade, drinking a cup of chilled orange tea, the breeze caresses my hair and brings with it the scents from the lantana and the sprawling rosemary nearby. I can't help but reflect on my life.

It's hard to believe that it wasn't all that long ago when I thought that my life was a disaster and that it would never change. I lived in constant physical pain, my personal and professional environments were full of negativity and melodrama, and I was lonely and scared.

Not anymore.

With a smiling heart, I recall the night that my dream of the flying cows first returned. Little did I know at the time how that dream, and all the subsequent ones, would transform my life—and how the dreams' profound messages and underlying wisdom would send me on a quest that has led me to this magical moment overlooking the lake.

As I close my eyes, I drift into a space between sleeping and waking. So much has happened since those days when the cows slept in the room below my bedroom with only some wooden planks separating us. I feel myself lifted by the warm breeze. Shadows drift over me. I am aware of my wise, friendly cows drifting overhead again. But this time it feels different. I am no longer a little girl looking up at them as they fly overhead. I am soaring with them!

Today, the little girl inside of me who somehow managed to steer those enormous, strong cows to the pasture and then home again gets to steer her life with the wisdom that her seven cows breathed into her.

Now I am a grown woman who has liberated herself from everything that held her down. I am free from everything that oppressed me—including pain and despair. I have the power to fly. I am surrounded by people I love and who love me, I am free from all the ghosts of the past, I live in a beautiful, peaceful place and I get to work at what feeds my heart and soul.

I am free to be my true self.

Higher and higher I soar. I feel light and joyful, frolicking in the calm sky with my beloved cows.

I don't know what my future may bring, but I know that, whatever it is, with the help of my cows I will handle it with grace—and I'll always be able to regain hope and seek new possibilities.

I am having so much fun because I know now that I can soar as high as my dreams will take me.

I am free.

Now, it's Your Turn...

Are you ready to soar as high as your dreams will take you?

Imagine your life a year from now. Imagine yourself embracing the real you, and all that makes you unique. You accept and nurture your gifts, talents, passions, and values. You own your story without concealing the less than attractive parts. You live your life placing greater importance on *who* you are, rather than on what you own, your resume, who you have by your side, and even what you wear.

How wonderful and liberating will it be to live your life with the emphasis on who you are inside!

Imagine knowing exactly what your heart is starving for, those core needs that it has been craving since you were a child. You have the secret code to what makes your heart feel full and satisfied and you trust it to point the way. You build a life for yourself where your heart is nourished every day.

How fulfilling and satisfying will it be when you focus more on feeling than on doing!

Imagine yourself being in control of that "committee" in your head. Your inner chatter and rants no longer hold you back when you should move forward, and they no longer have the power to propel you into the abyss when it's safer for you to stay put. You can remain grounded and optimistic—no matter where your thoughts and emotions try to take you. You are at peace.

How uplifting and freeing it will be to have the power to tame whatever steals your joy!

Imagine yourself being able to tap into your intuition whenever you want to and asking it to point you in the direction that is best for you—not what the rest of the world is doing or suggests you should do. Imagine a haven where you can retreat when you need a boost of goodness, where you can reconnect with your true essence, your inner light.

How enlightening will it be having access to your inner sun!

Imagine yourself free from all the boundaries that keep you boxed in. You adopt a spirit of adventure and let your inner child come out and play. You allow yourself to laugh and be silly and you bring levity and humor to all aspects of your life, including work and relationships. You give yourself license to enjoy life to the fullest.

How joyful and fun will it be when you add a touch of playful magic to everything you do!

Imagine yourself surrounded by people who elevate you, who honor your space, who are committed to your success and want the best for you. People who elevate your personal average. People who are positive influences in your life and are ready to open doors for you, guide you when you lose your way, or catch you when you fall. People who fill your well on a regular basis.

How refreshing and empowering will it be to have high-caliber relationships in your life!

Imagine yourself touching the lives of those around you in a positive way, leaving them in a better state than when you first interacted with them. You spread positivity. You are a force for good. You commit to a greater cause that improves the lives of others, in your home, your city, your country, our planet.

How rewarding, gratifying, and inspiring will your life be when you commit to helping others soar higher!

With these seven practices, you know you will be able to elevate yourself to higher ground. Trust them to lift you higher, to raise you above what is holding you back today. You don't have to remain on the hard ground looking up longingly at something you think is out of reach—*you can fly high!*

You have the power to create the life you dream about.

May the teachings from the Flying Cows dare you to soar to amazing new heights where your heart and soul are flying free.

ABOUT THE AUTHOR

As a master of transformation, Maria Rivera draws from all her knowledge and experiences in coaching, mentoring, psychology, human resources, spirituality, consulting, creative solutions, intuition, and management skills to offer everyone a way to take back control of their lives, break free from the debilitating judgment of others, and make meaningful change, whether in the workplace, in the community, or at home.

Professionally, Maria has made and remade herself multiple times. As a Hispanic immigrant woman, she faced numerous challenges as she climbed the corporate ladder and eventually found herself in a management role at Prudential Financial. She held multiple leadership positions before becoming vice president of change management, delivering benchmark strategies for large-scale change. With an extensive background in accounting, systems, operations, and human resources, she has helped organizations shift course from potential turmoil to work environments where employees feel inspired, engaged, and valued—all while delivering hundreds of millions in savings.

Maria is a mentor and coach, dedicated to creating growth opportunities for people of all kinds, from at-risk youth to aspiring professionals, and fostering their success, both inside and outside of the workplace. She has coached hundreds of women from disadvantaged groups who could not otherwise afford coaching. She also volunteers as a mentor to teenagers who come from families who don't speak English (Maria is fluent in English, Spanish, and Portuguese), whose parents are illegal in the country, or whose home life is toxic. Finally, Maria has also traveled to numerous developing countries in Asia and Latin America to help improve the lives of children stuck in poverty and illness. She is not afraid to look darkness in the face in order to ease the pain and suffering of others.

Through her own life experiences, Maria has learned that the key to transformation lies inside each of us, and her approach is therefore internal. She developed the Fly High Method as a way to help guide others through the process of reclaiming joy and agency in their lives by rejecting the often debilitating "shoulds and ought-tos" imposed by society, embracing one's true self, taking healthy risks with confidence, and listening to the heart.

It can be a long and bumpy road to a new life, but Maria and her seven cows are here to show you that it is possible—the hard work will pay off. Listen: they are even laughing.

You can connect with Maria

on her website: theflyingcows.com

LinkedIn at Maria Rivera

and on

Facebook, Instagram, and Twitter: FlyHighMethod

Made in the USA
San Bernardino, CA
03 November 2019